HUMANE RESOURCES

Bridging The Gap Between People and Profit

William J. Wiggins

Foreword

As the pages of 'Humane Resources' by William Wiggins unfold before you, it is important to note that this is not your typical book on human resources. This is a testament to the dynamic intersection of humanity and management, challenging traditional concepts of HR in favor of an approach that emphasizes human connection, empathy, and kindness.

Throughout his career, he has accumulated a wealth of knowledge and understanding about the intricacies of human interaction in the workplace. His experiences across industries, cultures, and corporate structures have informed his unique perspective. In this book, William shares insights to transform how we approach human resources and inspire a more compassionate, understanding, and effective corporate world.

'Humane Resources' places people at the core of every business strategy, every management decision, every recruitment process, and every corporate innovation. It boldly asserts that a company's greatest asset is its people and advocates for their nurturing and growth with the same rigor and diligence often reserved for financial resources and physical assets.

This book is a call to action: a plea for a new era of HR, where people are not seen as resources to be managed, but as unique individuals whose creativity, passion, and intelligence are the driving forces of success. It's about treating employees with empathy and respect, creating workplaces that foster personal and professional growth, and understanding that each person brings something unique and invaluable to the table.

Written with candor, humor, and profound wisdom, 'Humane Resources' is an exploration of what human resources can become when we allow our humanity to lead the way. William fosters an easy-to-grasp, conversational style that makes complex ideas digestible and inspiring, making it an invaluable guide for HR professionals, executives, managers, and anyone who believes in the transformative power of humanity in the workplace.

As you delve into 'Humane Resources,' you'll find that it's more than a book—it's a movement toward a more compassionate, humane way of working and living. A book that will challenge you, inspire you, and make you think differently.

Welcome to a journey that promises to reshape your perception of Human Resources.

-Chris Englin, CEO. Big Wave Recruiting –
Seattle Washington

ABOUT THE AUTHOR

William is an accomplished HR Consultant providing effective and professional HR leadership through Swift HR Solutions, Inc. Over the span of his career, William has gained a broad range of experience while leading HR teams representing all core HR disciplines vital to a profitable, sustainable organization: its employees; its internal management teams on matters including, but not limited to, HR compliance, employee benefits, and compensation, talent acquisition, performance management, organizational policies and workflows; and HR operations including implementation and management of integrated HRIS systems.

Through strategic HR roles at Mercer Human Resources Consulting, Kaiser Permanente, Williams-Sonoma, and other West Coast businesses, William has established a track record for building culture and engagement through leadership training and development. He is known as an industry leader when it comes to building strong collaborative HR partnerships and employee-focused leadership teams.

William has also led Diversity, Equity & Inclusion initiatives, and has studied abroad at the National University of Columbia, Bogota, and Gloucestershire University, Cheltenham, in the UK. He brings a broad perspective to his work and the clients that he serves. He also holds certifications in Gallup Strengthsfinder and Korn Ferry 360 Assessments, and is a Fierce Conversations training facilitator.

Dedication

I want to acknowledge the essential role that top journals such as Unleash.ai, CareerXroads, Recruiting News Network, the HR Gazette, and Fistful of Talent have played in providing me the opportunities and forums to share invaluable contexts and perspectives. The importance of these publications in producing this book cannot be overstated. They have not only been platforms that have embraced the most innovative HR ideologies but continue to serve as sources of knowledge supporting HR professionals globally in building great organizations.

To the unsung heroes of every corporation - the HR professionals who weave their magic behind the scenes. For their relentless dedication, for navigating the corridors of policies, bureaucracy, and most importantly, human emotions, and still emerging victorious.

To all my clients, guides, coaches, and colleagues at Swift HR Solutions, Inc., who remind me that the 'Human' in Human Resources is what truly matters.

And, most notably, to my own HR mentors, teams, and colleagues:

Martin Burns	Brian Powell
Dawn Chiasson	Suzanne Rodriguez
Gerry Crispin	Mel Royle
Chris Englin	Savanna Sissom
Barb Fives	Ericka Singh
Chris Frobel	Sean Stubblefield
Mike Harrington	Renee Swain
Chris Havrilla	Cleveland Tyson
Beth Hrdlicka	Melissa Willis
Andrea King	Ebonee Woods
Claire Lang	

Many of you saw the potential I didn't see in myself and taught me the value of empathy, resilience, patience, and the art of listening. You've shown me that the heart of any company isn't in its revenue or strategy but in its people.

Finally, to anyone who has ever felt unheard, underappreciated, or misunderstood in their place of work, this book is for you. Change is on the horizon.

– William Wiggins, Author

TABLE OF CONTENTS

CHAPTER 1

Human Resources

"WHEN I APPLIED HERE FOR THE ADVERTISED HUMAN RESOURCE POSITION I HAD NO IDEA THAT I WAS THE RESOURCE."

1. DISPELLING HR POLICE MYTHOLOGY

It was a mere five minutes before the clock struck 5:00 p.m. on a Friday evening. I found myself at my desk, engaging in a discussion about the sales team's plans for a happy hour event. In an unexpected turn of events, the HR representative emerged, metaphorically summoning me and a fellow Account Executive to attend a meeting in the realm of personnel affairs. You are likely wondering what initiated this summons. Well, the story goes like this:

Days earlier, during a marketing and sales team-building retreat held in Sedona, Arizona, my colleague and I came under scrutiny from the personnel facilitator. Our alleged transgression was failing to fully engage in an exercise that required us to delve into our deepest emotions. It was reported that we had expressed our incredulity through eye-rolling during a particularly unconventional task, where we were instructed to tap into our somber experiences and "let our tears flow." Subsequently, we were secluded together in a small, chilly office for a span exceeding an hour, before the entrance of the head of the Personnel department, who took on a rather authoritative stance.

This individual, often referred to as the "bad cop," was a towering figure, sporting a short-sleeved shirt, a clip-on tie, and high-waist Sansa belt slacks. We were given a stern warning about our perceived lack of team spirit, and we were informed that the incident had been reported to the CEO, elevating the matter to a higher echelon of concern.

The memory of this encounter still evokes a sense of exasperation within me, causing an involuntary roll of my eyes.

Ultimately, we were released without any formal charges, although not before being reminded of the gravity of our actions. As my partner in this escapade and I ascended in the elevator back up to the 35th floor to retrieve our personal belongings, I turned to her, witnessing her continued astonishment at the ordeal, and in a moment of frustration, I exclaimed, "This is exactly why I will NEVER work in Human Resources. Who do they think they are? The (expletive) police?" However, here I find myself now, a quarter-century later, situated right at the heart of what we more aptly call Human Resources.

Although Human Resources is not a new sector, certain persistent myths about this sector are difficult to debunk. These beliefs are founded, in part, on practices that have misrepresented the profession and situations that have left employees scared of Human Resources:

Myth #1 – HR is charged with policing employees.
Just because HR tends to be associated with policy enforcement, terminations, and disciplinary measures, some employees only see HR as enforcers (thus, the vow I took never to be caught dead in HR). I didn't want to work for a department whose primary purpose was to make people's lives unpleasant at work. In practice, Human Resources department is not the police; yet, when done well, Human Resources is an organization's most important instrument for studying its culture and determining how to sustain high engagement, low turnover, and good

morale. In order to minimize legal risks, HR is also responsible for managing compliance, aligning the right people with effective roles, and ensuring that leadership is knowledgeable about legal issues related to employment. HR priorities often don't include listening for swearing or looking for eye-rolling during a team-building exercise.

Myth #2 – HR exists to protect the organization, not the employees.

According to surveys, 72% of those who participated consider their HR department to be the "puppet" of the executive team. HR is responsible for disseminating important change management and policy information. Additionally, they are in charge of standing out for the rights of employees involved in disputes or issues at work. The human resources department can act as a neutral facilitator or, if required, an advocate for employees if there is a problem that is harming employee engagement or productivity or if the workforce is not receiving a new policy. Calling attention to poor management or unethical hiring practices that have a negative effect on employees can sometimes be considered "protecting" a business.

Myth #3 – HR cannot be trusted to keep confidence.

It is the responsibility of HR to gauge an organization's health and share the results. A company's entire culture, how employees are treated, or how they support the goal, vision, and values of the company, is evaluated by HR. To fulfill important business goals and objectives, your HR staff must evaluate what is working, what is not working, and what needs to change. In order to handle more serious issues like harassment, discrimination, bullying, etc., an HR professional may occasionally be required to communicate an employee's concerns and follow up on complaints with management. If an employee is having a problem, HR should offer both assistance and representation. However, be aware that HR might need to include others in order to find a solution.

Myth #4 – Human Resources adds no revenue value to an organization.
Due to the misconception that we cannot provide measurable financial data about our workload, we do not generate revenue, and our HR projects and programs do not yield noticeable results, the field of human resources is occasionally referred to as "soft. "Really? With the de-ployment of HR scorecards, the times are changing, as seen by the growing significance of controlling and re-porting staff turnover and top talent defection rates. Not to mention that it is possible to quantify the reduction in absenteeism against engagement, safety incident costs, overall headcount, competitiveness in pay and benefits, the number of employees who have received training, HR expenses as a share of operating expenses, internal customer satisfaction, low time-to-fill ratios, and cost per hire. There is no doubt that HR plays a role in the overall profitability and revenue of a firm.

In conclusion, HR must be part of the broader business strategy of an organization and have a place at the table when establishing and prioritizing strategic business goals that go far beyond employee policing. To be effective in improving the general performance of the company, HR must have the full support of the whole organization, from the top down.

2. HR TRANSFORMATION: NO TIME LIKE THE PRESENT

As an HR professional, you are fully aware of the following situation: An employee in the break room approaches you and inquires whether you are the new Human Resources Manager. As soon as you say yes, you learn that the employee is having some difficulties. You console her, encourage her to work, and then let her leave. But then you realize you're not helping the business or the HR team by acting as a counselor, resolving benefits issues, and advising mature employees on how to behave. You decide to strengthen your HR department by considering how to operate at a more strategic level rather than just operational and functional levels.

So, what exactly is HR transformation?

Human Resource transformation entails reframing human resources as an essential component of an organization's key business strategies. It investigates methods to strengthen the department's basic tasks in order to make HR more advising and influential, resulting in a more productive and cost-efficient company. Human Resources has evolved throughout time, from the conventional "personnel" enforcement and compliance arm of the corporation to a more strategic discipline. Today, HR departments manage tasks as broad as identifying and retaining top people, managing change, and developing and sustaining a healthy, inclusive workplace culture - all of which reinforce an organization's core basis. If HR is to maintain its seat at the strategic leadership table, we must provide our leaders with a more imaginative manner to help the company. In short, HR Transformation!

Five Strategic HR Transformation Initiatives

As part of their HR strategy, every firm should consider or improve on the following five HR transformation initiatives:

1. **Strive to become data-driven**

   If an HR Dashboard is not officially in place, it is suggested that it be implemented as soon as possible this fiscal year. Consider implementing a monitoring platform that aggregates statistics relevant to critical HR indicators, with a particular emphasis on measures linked with the company's objectives and financial advantages. The dashboard should provide visual representations of data that aid in improving recruiting methods, fine-tuning workplace administration, and increasing staff efficiency. Track a set of 8 to 10 key indicators that will serve as performance benchmarks, as well as measures that will be relevant to future organizational successes.

2. **Create an internal partnership that aligns with your business goals**

Ensure that HR is represented in the leadership forum and train your whole HR team to take a consultative approach rather than purely transactional relationships. Improve your HR Team's capabilities and reputation as capable experts who work closely with recruiting managers and senior executives. This collaborative approach strives to develop strategies for recruiting, pay, employee engagement, and talent management that are in sync with the overall corporate goals. Begin by discussing your senior leadership cohort's objectives, and then devise ways for leveraging the power of your HR staff to aid in achieving these aspirations.

3. **Invest in technology**

To improve all aspects of the employment life-cycle, from recruiting to operations to turn-over, the Human Resources department must be equipped with cutting-edge data-gathering systems that work at peak efficiency. Strategic use of HR technology helps the recruitment, acquisition, retention, and development of people while also streamlining workforce administration. Furthermore, it provides organizational leaders with critical decision-making resources, improving the efficacy of HR-related decisions. The achievement of these goals necessitates the use of cutting-edge technology with remarkable functionality.

4. **Automate core transactional processes**

The pivotal transformation of HR from a transactional function to a strategic enabler hinges on the automation of fundamental procedures. The augmentation of employee empowerment via self-service attributes translates into a proportional allocation of your valuable time toward nurturing a fortified and resilient organizational culture. Your existing HR systems likely possess the capacity to automate a broader spectrum of processes than is presently utilized. This juncture could prove opportune for an evaluation of your Human Resources Information System (HRIS).

5. **Start thinking three steps ahead**

Strategic progress is hindered by an excessive focus on short-term considerations. Such a perspective only addresses immediate challenges, analogous to extinguishing fires. A more balanced mid-term outlook, however, delves into the root causes of issues. Yet, the ultimate goal should be the fortification of the entire structure against potential threats. By adopting a forward-thinking approach, envisioning several steps ahead, you will seamlessly align HR with the broader organizational strategy, thereby advancing toward the coveted role of a strategic business partner.

In the realm of Human Resources, change remains a steadfast constant, necessitating proactive measures to remain ahead of the curve. Embracing the transformation of HR and reevaluating the operational dynamics of your HR team positions you optimally to facilitate adaptation and growth for your organization, its leadership, hiring managers, and workforce. Above all, such transformation invariably culminates in the cultivation of a more progressive and competitive corporate entity.

3. HUMAN RESOURCES: ACHIEVING THE RIGHT BALANCE OF HEAD VS. HEART

I received a crash course a few years ago on the value of treating employees with both heart and mind while providing them with service. I'd had a few friendly conversations with a specific employee as I went about my HR duties. We shared our mutual love of southern cuisine and travel, and, as always, talked about our dreams of retiring someday. We also argued over the best places to eat in San Francisco, where we had both lived at differ-ent times.

The employee's admission that he was having throat and abdominal pain one day gave our discussions additional significance. I didn't feel particularly concerned, but I asked the standard HR questions, such as "Do you need accommodation, time off, or FMLA?" I advised the employee to take some time for self-care and to make the most of the fantastic benefits that the organization offers.

After a certain period of time, the employee's supervisor reported to me that he was having attendance problems and facing possible disciplinary action. Keeping in mind the earlier chat, I contacted the employee to see if there was anything we could do to help him. It was at that point that I discovered he had esophageal cancer. This time, in response to my standard HR queries, "Do you need accommodation, time off, or FMLA?" he said, "Yes, I think it's time." I advised the manager to forgo the disciplinary action. Additionally, I gave the employee advice to put himself and his family first, to keep me updated, and to let HR manage the "head" things (the administration of his benefits and leave activity). I reassured him that I would be there as a source of assistance, motivator, and confidante. I consulted the benefits staff on FMLA eligibility, calculating PTO balances, and giving the employee all the required documentation so that his time and employment were safeguarded. In order for the employee to prepare for the fight of his life, our leave team assisted him with the short-term disability process and qualification, confirmed his deductibles, copays, and coinsurance amounts, and connected him with his carrier to confirm specialist provider participation and coverage. I questioned:

- How else can the organization support him?

- What is his FMLA balance?

- Does our life insurance coverage have an accelerated benefits rider?

- Does he have a designated beneficiary?

- What resources through our Employee Assistance Plan might be useful?

- Might he at some point need a reasonable accommodation?

- Was there a contingency plan to support his job in his absence?

- Will he be returning at all?

Months later, the employee entered my office and informed me that his illness had advanced to stage 4. I closed the door, sat down next to him, and stretched out my hand. He tightened his grasp on it and started to cry. I spent nearly an hour watching him break down. No conference call or meeting was more significant than that time spent with him. I had to be there, at that moment, with "heart." It was difficult not to cry with him, but it was his time.

Again, the employee, a mere shell of his former self, returned for a visit. "The doctor thinks I probably won't make it to Christmas," he muttered as he turned to face me. It was stunning to hear someone talk so casually of their mortality with such brave conviction. However, he was worried about money in these last few months, which meant I needed to serve using my head to figure out how I and my team could best support him. I explained to the employee that the organization offered an Accelerated Death Benefit that would enable him to use the money from his policy before passing away to aid with expenditures. He was unaware of that benefit, nor had he thought about his retirement funds, which he could use without paying penalties because of his age. I also reminded him that our Employee Assistance Plan could support him and his family with additional end-of-life planning services, and I connected him to our EAP representative.

I stood hesitantly as he left my office that day. I had a gut feeling it was the last time I would see him alive. I'd made certain the employee had access to all the tools needed to follow up with the life insurance retirement plan and EAP suppliers. I said goodbye to him in the lobby, we hugged, (completely appropriate under the circumstances) and whispered to a family member who was waiting there to keep me informed and then I withdrew to my office for a moment. A few weeks later I received news from the family member that the employee had died. I could only hope that, with the right balance of heart and mind, I and my team had given the employee all the necessary Human Resources as well as emotional support as he neared the most important life event of all.

4. HOMELESSNESS IN THE WORKPLACE: IT HAPPENS

I had the most conscientious of administrative assistants. He was always enthusiastic, always on time, an expert with PowerPoint, and skilled at simplifying procedures. He was college-educated, and by all accounts, never had a bad day. He was also homeless. This discovery was made by following several hints. Always a little wrinkled, yet appropriate, always groomed, but just barely; and always binged workplace snacks, frequently taking any leftovers at the end of the day. Although I was well aware that he had a backstory, neither his look nor his conduct violated any explicit HR policies.

One night after work, while picking up groceries for dinner, I saw him behind a local business next to a car, which I later discovered was his temporary home. Loaded with what appeared to be personal items, I called out his name. When he turned to face me, I saw what can only be described as defeat and shame. He was homeless. I asked him to accompany me while I went shopping. The idea was to do some shopping for him while also shopping for myself, so I told him to get whatever items he needed, my treat. As we strolled with a cart, I joked with him that it was in place of the Christmas bonus he had not received the year before. He described to me his journey to homelessness throughout our outing, which culminated with a landlord who didn't inform him that his house was in foreclosure until the day of the eviction, heartbreaking but very realistic.

Before leaving with our groceries, we arranged to hunker down in a conference room the next day to look at options for getting him to a better place.

a. **Contributing wage and income factors**

Contrary to popular opinion, the vast majority of minimum and low-wage employees are working adults. Wage stagnation and decline have put housing alternatives out of reach for many employees, especially those who live and work in cities or areas where the cost of living and inflation outpace yearly merit and cost of living increases. According to recent research referenced by Melinda Giovengo PhD, Chief Executive Officer of Youth Care in Seattle, Washington, every $100 increase in rent directly connects to a 15% increase in homelessness in the Seattle Metropolitan area, where rents increased by more than 3.4% in February 2017. Even when the economy recovered after the recession, yearly pay adjustments remained 1%-2% ahead of inflation in any given year. Employees have a low expectation of receiving a cost-of-living adjustment. Outstanding employees earn a 5% rise on average, which is only slightly more than their typical colleagues, who received a 3.1% raise in 2016, which, while welcome, may not be enough to make a substantial economic difference. So, is it feasible that a moderately compensated admin, living paycheck to paycheck, without a support structure, and in one of America's most expensive cities, with no savings, may wind up couch surfing, or worse? Absolutely!

b.   Resources to consider

Implementing an Employee Assistance Fund is a commendable initiative. In the event that your company enjoys profitability, it's an opportune moment to give back to your employee community. This can be achieved by establishing a fund designed to provide financial aid to employees facing genuine hardships, subject to specific qualifying criteria.

Additionally, consider instituting a Payroll Advance Program aimed at facilitating timely assistance to employees confronted with unexpected circumstances. This scheme enables eligible individuals to obtain advances on their payroll, offering a practical means to alleviate financial burdens during challenging times.

Establish a strategic partnership with an effective Employee Assistance Program (EAP). EAPs were traditionally connected with assisting employees suffering from difficulties like addiction, mental health concerns, or personal disputes. However, modern full-service EAPs have grown to provide a greater range of services. These now include assistance in discussing personal issues, ranging from work-related transitions to legal counsel and financial advice, among other things.

As a key practice, include regular and thoughtful involvement with your staff. Keep a close eye on their health and performance. If you notice any signs of personal or professional barriers to their success, address them with care, respect, and conformity to legal rules. Develop the skills to deal with such difficulties in a way that respects both the dignity and legal rights of employees.

The most essential thing is to supervise your employees without passing judgment and to maintain open channels of communication so that they feel free to discuss any issues that may affect their ability to give their all at work and home. Although you are not expected to be a social worker, having compassion and empathy are essential traits for a leader since they will help an employee in need and eventually improve your company's bottom line.

5. FOSTERING A SAFE WORKPLACE DURING POLITICALLY CHARGED TIMES

Whether in a video conference room, an online chat, or the break room, passionate and intense conversations may (and will) occur. The conversation may be enlightening and challenging, but it may also stray off into unsettling terrain. It's not always easy to distinguish between a hostile workplace and the right to free expression. Even though our First Amendment right to free speech is protected in public institutions and local governments, it is not in the majority of private businesses, unless your staff members are employed in one of the few states where political membership is a protected class. When does political diversity among coworkers become a disadvantage, even if it may be constructive and educational? How can it be controlled and compared against one's right to free expression guaranteed by the Constitution?

Tips for fostering a safe workplace

As we approach one of the most politically heated eras of our history, here are some suggestions for keeping a cohesive, secure, and productive work environment for all, regardless of whether your employee's favorite political hero is red, white, black, or even orange:

- **First and foremost, promote a culture of respect from the top down**

It's important to recognize that everyone has the right to retain certain opinions and values, regardless of an employee's position, whether they work in the C-Suite or at the front desk. It is our responsibility to establish an environment free from intimidation and fear that encourages an open and courteous exchange of ideas.

Meaningful conversations may be fostered by creating a workplace where people feel free to voice their opinions without fear of retaliation. Such candid discussions are essential to the development of a progressive organization because they enable the interchange of various viewpoints and ideas.

- **Proceed with caution**

  It is critical to have a firm grasp of your team. Participating in political debates at work might be dangerous. Employees who are facing disciplinary action or termination may correlate these repercussions with irrelevant statements or thoughts aired during a heated political debate. As a result, people may claim that they are being targeted or shunned.

  While encouraging open communication is essential for team engagement, it is also critical to remember that how you communicate is just as important, if not more important, than what you convey. Being aware of the tone, context, and manner in which political discussions take place can assist in preventing misunderstandings and the possibility of employees feeling unfairly treated or ostracized.

- **Know when enough is enough**

  It is vital to train employees to pay attention to social cues and recognize when their teammates are feeling uneasy in an environment that supports polite discourse. It is your responsibility as a leader to be vigilant and to act when necessary.

  If a conversation turns into rivalry, rudeness, or a threat, as a leader, do not be hesitant to interfere and redirect the conversation. Maintaining a healthy and inclusive workplace culture necessitates that conversations remain respectful and polite.

- **Review your policies for consistent**

  As the election season approaches, it's a good time to review our corporate policy on electronic communications, harassment, cultural sensitivity, and even our dress code. We acknowledge that many opinions and ideas exist inside our business, and we support each employee's freedom to have and express their own.

  However, it is critical to underline that our rules on these topics are in place to create an inclusive, courteous, and thoughtful environment for all workers and customers. While wearing a "Make America Great Again" t-shirt and accessories may be a means of self-expression for individuals, we should be aware that it may send a message that contradicts our intended professional image.

We encourage every employee to express their own opinions tactfully and sensitively, whether through dress or technological correspondence. Any type of harassment or discrimination will not be accepted. All of our workers are expected to have conversations that promote mutual respect and understanding because we appreciate open and courteous communication.

The goals of our dress code guidelines are to preserve a professional image that is consistent with our organizational values and client expectations. As we navigate this election season, we appreciate your understanding and help in respecting these standards. Your adherence to these rules helps to create a welcoming and peaceful workplace for everyone.

- **Remember your role as an employer**

    Your dedication to creating a safe and comfortable working environment is unwavering. It is critical to emphasize that the First Amendment does not free you of the responsibility of creating clear standards and limitations for political discussions among our personnel. Furthermore, you are responsible for addressing and mitigating disturbances that may impede your organization's growth, even if those interruptions are the result of political disputes.

We truly think that political debates in the workplace can be done in a way that is consistent with our values of respect, inclusivity, and sensitivity. These characteristics are essential for establishing a progressive organization. We support free discourse and debate as long as it is handled with mutual respect and understanding.

By establishing clear standards and cultivating an environment that prioritizes courteous and thoughtful communication, you can guarantee that political conversations inside your organization are both productive and in line with your commitment to progress.

6. HR BURNOUT: THE NEW PANDEMIC

No, it's not your imagination. HR burnout is real. Human Resources professionals, by nature of the business, are typically charged with meeting the needs of everyone else with perseverance. While powering through and perseverance is noble, it can be emotionally and mentally exhausting. Have you:

- reached an all-time low in your mental health, feeling overwhelmed, emotionally exhausted, and unable to fulfill incessant demands?

- felt that your life has been reduced to administrative tasks?

- felt challenged and unmotivated as a result of the HR functions and, to some extent, your lack of prioritization?

- grown bored with your job?

- seen a decline in your inventiveness, with poor judgment, impatience, and irritation as your default responses to internal clients and colleagues?

- had a few weeping fits and a sore throat for good measure?

"DON'T PANIC – YOU ARE NOT ALONE!"

In reality, you and numerous other HR professionals are both exhibiting identical symptoms. The reason? **'HR burnout'** is a metaphorical virus that has lately gained notoriety and is rapidly spreading to pandemic levels. Although there is no vaccination available for this, the good news is that there haven't been any confirmed fatalities either. Over the past two years, as the globe has been engulfed in a pandemic unlike any other, the burden for HR directors and their teams has expanded enormously.

To assist their organization's human capital during school closings, decreased work hours, and external stresses affecting their jobs, such as sickness and death, HR executives and their teams were designated as "essential staff" and given the responsibility of modifying workspaces, policies, and benefits.

We were tasked with leading our organization's efforts to improve mental health to combat new challenges such as social isolation, Zoom fatigue, survivors' remorse, grief, childcare, adult care, a reduction in their household income, and a variety of other issues that had suddenly become a part of an employee's new reality. HR professionals helped their organizations navigate uncharted territory as they learned to navigate unfamiliar terrain due to the pandemic, all while struggling with many of the same issues as the rest of the organization and being unable to prioritize their health and well-being. Over the course of two years dedicated to assisting organizations in achieving their goals in remote work settings, and in our never-ending pursuit of sustaining employee morale and eliminating obstacles to peak performance, it has become clear that burnout among HR professionals is a very real and particularly acute concern.

Why is HR burnout particularly severe?

One of the few departments in a business that reports to senior leadership as well as workers is Human Resources. Prior to the pandemic, HR departments were already having trouble keeping up with the mounting demands. COVID-19 just fueled the fire. Our working environments also altered as a result of the pandemic, and the success of companies depended on how fast and effectively they could adapt, which necessitated the adoption of new procedures and policies. The ability of HR teams to learn and execute, frequently simultaneously, swiftly, and effectively determined how fast firms could react.

The emergence of what has been labeled the 'Great Resignation' created enormous issues. By 2021, HR leaders were forced to consider structural changes to satisfy their businesses' changing demands. Talent acquisition teams were dealing with rising competition for a shrinking talent pool, as well as high retention rates and the need to replace essential posts that had become empty.

The results of a poll performed by Work Ivo, an Ireland-based workplace communication software, which included over 500 HR experts from the United States and the United Kingdom, showed that HR workers were struggling. An astounding 98% of HR workers cited exhaustion and strain, with 94% reporting feeling overwhelmed. Surprisingly, just 29% of individuals polled stated that their businesses actually valued their efforts.

To compound these difficulties, an increasing number of HR directors are dealing with a scarcity of critical resources, leaving them without the tools and assistance they need to carry out their responsibilities successfully. In light of these unique circumstances, it has never been more important for HR professionals to prioritize self-care.

What is an HR professional to do?

Go back to the basics; simply say, it is that easy. Consider pausing to think about what influences your job satisfaction—or lack thereof—and how you may approach your work differently. The only environment that HR professionals can alter well enough to meet their demands is other environments.

Ignite the healing process with a few simple changes:

It is critical to recognize and resolve compassion fatigue. We've seen staff struggle with tremendous emotional lows, one after the other, over the last two years. It is critical for every one of us to understand the significance of compassion fatigue in our job and to be aware of its causes. Detecting it in real time enables more effective control of its consequences.

Another important step is setting boundaries. There was a huge requirement for HR's fast answers and attention at the height of the epidemic. We could have unintentionally encouraged the belief that HR should be accessible round-the-clock in our haste to help. The truth is that not many HR-related events qualify as emergencies. It's time to intentionally create boundaries and modify this view. It's critical to understand that if our mental health is affected, we are not only failing our business and coworkers but also ourselves. Making our health a priority is a crucial component of efficient HR management.

Recognizing burnout is the first step, and it's critical to be open about your need for help. Working remotely, in the office, or using a mixed method requires you to disengage from work without feeling guilty. Burnout is not a fabrication of your imagination, and it demands our respect and care. There is no bravery in persevering. It's critical to follow your own advice in the same empathetic spirit in which you tell them to take the time they need.

Take advantage of every opportunity to recharge, whether it's a well-deserved vacation or a few sick days. No HR professional should be afraid to confess burnout, and it is far better to address it proactively than to let it take control.

Change is constant in the ever-changing HR sector, and the demands placed on HR staff are always changing. Burnout is a common problem that many HR professionals must deal with; it's neither an isolated problem nor a criticism of your skills. The good news is that services for helping you manage burnout are sprouting up quickly. Utilize these resources and place a high priority on your health if you want to continue productively serving your company and coworkers.

CHAPTER 2

Employee Engagement

"YOUR EMPLOYEES HAVE LOST FAITH IN YOUR
ABILITY TO PRETEND TO CARE ABOUT THEM."

1. WORKPLACE BULLYING: THE NEW NORMAL

At the age of thirteen, a significant epiphany unfolded in my life. The year was 1976, and picture me, an eighth grader, sporting a pair of light blue Converse All-Stars, boasting the perfect afro, and confidently navigating the halls of Canterbury Jr. High School. It was during this year that I experienced an encounter that would become my most legendary tale, one that some recount even to this day.

The central character in this story is Clifford, a classmate and neighbor who, by all accounts, should have been a sophomore in high school. Clifford had a considerable physical advantage over me, being two years older and nearly 80 pounds heavier. He had earned a reputation as the town's resident bully, and, for reasons known only to him, he had decided that I needed to be brought down a notch. Perhaps it was because I was popular, or maybe it was due to the fact that my older brother, Zedrick, was the town's star athlete and legendarily popular. Regardless, Clifford had taken issue with me, and the cafeteria was the battleground he chose.

Our clash began when Clifford, in an attempt to assert dominance, demanded that I vacate the seat across from him so he could put his substantial feet up. I, however, stood my ground and steadfastly refused to yield. In response, he flung a fruit cocktail in my direction. Not one to be outdone, I retaliated by launching a sloppy joe sandwich right back at him, followed by the entire tray. What followed was a showdown of epic proportions as we grappled and tussled, with me clinging on for dear life during the tumultuous ride that ensued.

That epiphany was transformative. I realized that my disdain for bullies ran deep. I'd much rather face the consequences of a threat than be subjected to someone's domination. It would be years before I encountered another bona fide bully, but this time, it was in my workplace, and the bully held a position of authority – my boss.

My boss was unapologetically a bully, openly endorsing a military-style command-and-control approach. He frequently expressed his dislike for people and his willingness to backfill every team member if necessary. It felt like déjà vu, a replay of the fruit cocktail and sloppy joe sandwich incident from my school days. Despite his attempts at intimidation and his reliance on fear tactics, I resisted him at every turn. However, I was acutely aware of the negative impact our adversarial relationship had on the team and the organization as a whole.

This experience reinforced my commitment to fostering an environment where individuals can work freely, unleash their creativity, and do so without fear, particularly when it comes to their colleagues and, most importantly, their boss.

What is a workplace bully?

A bully, as defined, is someone who repeatedly seeks to harm or intimidate individuals they perceive as vulnerable. If you've encountered such an individual within your organization, it signifies a significant problem.

Workplace bullying can be attributed to either an individual's behavior or a company culture that tolerates or perpetuates negative conduct. Research indicates that workplace bullies are predominantly male, and often, the bully holds a position of authority, such as a manager or supervisor. Typically, the bully either feels threatened by their target or lacks emotional intelligence.

Workplace bullying affects productivity and can result in significant costs for businesses. When the conduct crosses the line into harassment or hostility, these costs appear as greater turnover rates, increased absenteeism, and legal fees. Recognizing and dealing with workplace bullying is critical for sustaining a healthy and effective workplace.

Workplace bullying often encompasses situations where one or more individuals within the workplace single out another person, subjecting them to unjustifiably abusive or intimidating treatment. Typically, targets of workplace bullying are independent and competent employees who refuse to assume a subservient role. Paradoxically, they may be well-liked, socially adept, and inclined to avoid confrontations, which are all characteristics that can make them a target for workplace bullies.

It's worth noting that many employers lack a specific anti-bullying policy or may struggle to clearly define such behavior. Consequently, incidents of bullying are only reported approximately 38% of the time. This underreporting underscores the need for organizations to develop comprehensive anti-bullying policies and promote a workplace culture that fosters open communication and addresses such issues promptly and effectively.

Identifying a workplace bully

A "tough" or demanding manager can set high standards without resorting to abusive conduct. Such managers establish high standards while remaining courteous and fair in their approach to meeting them. Workplace bullying, on the other hand, includes the abuse or misuse of authority, which leaves employees feeling helpless and lonely. Bullying frequently comprises the following acts and behaviors:

- Shouting or swearing at an employee
- Verbal abuse targeted at an employee
- Being singled out for unjustified criticism or blame
- Being excluded/ socially isolated
- Being threatened with termination
- Misrepresenting an employee's job performance or contribution

- Excessive micro-managing or being given unrealistic deadlines
- Having your work or contributions purposefully ignored
- Actions that embarrass or humiliate

Indeed, it's crucial to differentiate between bullying and harassment, as they represent distinct categories of behavior, particularly in the context of the United States where legal protections exist. While both involve negative actions, harassment crosses a legal threshold and is considered unlawful when it is based on an individual's gender, ethnicity, religion, sexual orientation, disability, or other legally protected status.

The key distinction lies in the legality of the actions. Harassment is illegal and grants the victim legal rights to halt the behavior, seek recourse, and file complaints with relevant authorities or agencies. Individuals and organizations need to be aware of these legal boundaries and ensure that their workplaces are free from both bullying and harassment, as fostering a respectful and inclusive environment is not only ethically sound but also legally mandated.

How Workplace Bullying Impacts Your Employee

The Workplace Bullying Institute's online poll in 2017 revealed the following concerning findings:

- 19% of Americans are bullied, another 19% witness it

- 61% of Americans are aware of abusive conduct in the workplace
- It affects 60.4 million Americans
- 70% of perpetrators are men; 60% of targets are women
- 61% of bullies are bosses, and the majority (63%) operate alone
- 40% of bullied targets are believed to suffer adverse health effects
- 29% of targets remain silent about their experiences
- 71% of employer reactions are harmful to targets
- 60% of coworker reactions are harmful to targets
- 65% of targets lose their jobs in trying to stop it
- 46% report worsening of work relationships, post-Trump election

Employees subjected to bullying often exhibit reduced work commitment, disengagement, job insecurity, increased absenteeism, and greater reliance on leave benefits. Furthermore, a substantial 40% of targeted employees report stress-related health problems such as headaches, chronic neck pain, diabetes, sleep apnea, anxiety, depression, suicidal thoughts, and post-traumatic stress syndrome.

Despite resembling behavior seen in middle school, workplace bullying is, unfortunately, on the rise across various regions, from Washington DC to the Mexican border and beyond. This trend comes at a considerable cost to both your organization and its employees. To address this issue, consider involving your HR team in a workplace assessment, conducting pulse surveys, and implementing a strict anti-bullying policy with zero tolerance. Proactive measures like these can significantly contribute to fostering a culture of engagement and emotional well-being for all members of your organization.

2. HAVE YOU ENGAGED YOUR MILLENNIALS?

I once encountered a millennial employee in the copy room who was visibly distressed. He was frantically working to reduce and scan a nearly mural-sized floor plan requested by an executive two floors above, with an ASAP deadline looming. However, he was struggling to figure out how to efficiently shrink and email the document.

As time passed, his frustration escalated, almost to the point of tears. That's when I intervened and asked, "Does this really need to be scanned and emailed, or could you simply deliver it in person, the way it used to be done in the past?" He looked at me as if a heavenly choir had just sung, and calmly replied, "I guess I could do that."

In my close interactions with millennials in a managerial capacity, I've observed that problem-solving without relying on technology can be a significant challenge, especially for those who primarily rely on technology for communication. Millennials have grown up with technology as a fundamental means of connecting with others. While this can be an asset in many situations, they may not be as adept at handling communication that necessitates a more direct and personal approach.

As much as I disagree with stereotypes and believe that employees should not be judged based on when they were born, certain stereotypes are based on truth, and we can't ignore the fact that there are measurable differences among employees based on a variety of factors, including when they were born and how they were taught to learn:

- Millennials   born   1981-1996   represent   56 million in workforce
Generation X   born   1965-1980   represent   53 million in workforce
- Baby boomers born   1946-1964   represent   41 million in workforce

Understanding the differences among your various workforce generations can greatly facilitate effective management. A well-rounded workplace includes healthy representation from all generations but given that millennials have been the largest generation in the workforce since 2017, it's beneficial to focus on strategies for engaging them. If you haven't honed your skills in communicating with millennials, now is an opportune time to begin.

First and foremost, it's essential to shift your perspective. The workplace has evolved, and as managers, we must assist millennial employees in harnessing and leveraging their advanced technology skills while also identifying opportunities for them to develop new skills. This can be achieved by frequently assigning new projects or providing shadowing opportunities that challenge them, both personally and professionally, pushing them beyond their comfort zones. millennial employees seek a sense of purpose and meaning in their work that transcends financial gain. Yes, it may sound unconventional, but they aspire to see beyond the immediate horizon, often relying on your guidance to help them get there.

Be prepared to step into the roles of coach and mentor, even if these were not initially part of your career aspirations. Employees who do not have a positive relationship with their leaders are more likely to leave their positions, a trend particularly pronounced among millennials. Retention should become a key focus on your management dashboard. You'll need to develop a robust retention strategy like never before. Plan for more frequent career conversations beyond the annual performance review and conduct personal exit interviews with departing employees to gain insights into what went wrong and how to improve moving forward.

It's important to recognize that millennials have a strong desire for approval and validation from others. They are not driven by power or intimidation; instead, they thrive under leaders who are approachable and available to offer encouragement and guidance throughout their careers.

Moreover, it's essential to relax and acknowledge the generation gap that exists between millennials and older generations, especially concerning work processes and organizational structures. This gap can sometimes create the perception that millennials are less diligent. While older generations often value fixed work schedules, core hours, formal attire like collared shirts and ties, and adherence to traditional office norms, millennials tend to prioritize outcomes over conventional routines. In truth, millennials are hardworking and possess remarkable technical skills. With the right leadership, they can excel in ways that were not available to previous generations. Denim attire, for example, should not be seen as the enemy. Many millennials believe that their personal appearance is not relevant to their job performance and advocate for the option to work remotely, either occasionally or exclusively, as long as they deliver results. To attract and retain millennials, consider reevaluating traditional notions of professionalism and productivity.

Millennial employees value flexibility and autonomy in their work. They prefer not to be bound by strict eight-hour office schedules and are less committed to in-person collaboration than previous generations. Aim to create a more progressive and denim-friendly work environment that offers flexible work schedules and a less rigid dress code, one that ditches ties and synthetic blend slacks in favor of a focus on results rather than fashion.

Are you ready to disrupt?

I understand that managing millennials can be difficult, but it can also be a chance for managers to break the mold and create an effective cultural shift that leads to a more progressive firm. Make the most of the fact that millennials are here to stay.

3. EMPLOYER BRANDING'S VALUE TO HR

"Employer brand" refers to an employer's reputation as a good place to work and their employee value proposition, as opposed to the more generic corporation brand reputation and customer value proposition – Wikipedia Employer branding has progressed from a fashionable term with good intentions, to a key component of an organization's strategic growth strategy. Is there, however, a measurable talent management benefit to corporate branding?

What is considered a "strong" employer brand?

A strong employer brand is more than just a pretty face; it improves your company's reputation both inside and outside. It represents a clear goal statement or value proposition that forms an intrinsic element of the identity of your organization. A great employer brand is deeply established in your organization's culture and behaviors, whether it's a commitment to excellent customer service, a culture of compassion, or a focus on workers' well-being.

When employer branding is consistently and authentically practiced at every level of the organization, it can significantly enhance your company's appeal and bolster your ability to retain top talent. Ignoring employer branding in today's competitive job market essentially implies that your company's reputation is not a crucial factor in attracting and keeping talent or in creating a positive and engaging employee experience. In a world where talent acquisition and retention are paramount, nurturing a strong employer brand is an essential strategic move.

Why should you care about employer branding?

The importance of employer branding cannot be overstated, as it can be the decisive factor in swiftly and effectively hiring essential professionals such as nurses, project managers, or coders. A strong employer brand can attract top talent to your organization, ensuring that you don't lose them to the competition.

Moreover, employer branding can significantly impact turnover rates. It can mean the difference between having a single-digit turnover, which is favorable for organizational stability, and facing a double-digit turnover, which can disrupt operations and hinder growth.

Still uncertain about whether to incorporate an employer branding strategy into your talent management efforts in

2020? Consider the following potential benefits for your organization:

- **A good reputation can be profitable**

   While compensation remains an important consideration for job candidates, there is a notable shift away from money being the sole or primary factor in their job-seeking and employment decisions. CareerBuilder's data indicates that a significant portion of candidates, specifically 67%, would be willing to accept lower pay if the company they were interested in had positive reviews and a favorable reputation. This demonstrates that job seekers are increasingly valuing factors beyond salary, such as company culture, reputation, and employee experiences when evaluating potential employment opportunities.

- **Attracting and retaining the right talent**

   A significant majority of job seekers, about 78%, actively research a company's reputation as an employer before even applying for a job. Among Millennials, 88% consider being part of the right company culture as a top priority. This underscores the immense importance of maintaining a strong employer brand that potential applicants can access easily. It enables them to assess how well they might fit into your organization.

To effectively communicate your employer brand, it is critical to leverage social media platforms such as LinkedIn, Twitter, Facebook, and Instagram. This is because 79% of job seekers are likely to use social media during their job search. These platforms are among the most commonly used channels for job seekers to gather information and insights about prospective employers.

- **Closing time to fill gaps**

  You can attract more people and recruit faster by investing in employer branding. One of the primary advantages of having a great employer brand is having a broader talent pool from which to fill openings.

- **Higher engagement = lower turnover**

  Employer branding is more than simply encouraging talent, it's also a great tool for connecting with prospective workers before, during, and after the recruitment and onboarding process. This method greatly aids in the retention of critical staff. Indeed, organizations that engage in employer branding often see a 28% reduction in workforce turnover.

A strong employer brand may help you attract skilled applicants who are truly interested in your company, looking beyond superficial considerations and searching for a long-term commitment. This implies that you are less likely to have immediate attrition among your new hires. Furthermore, applicants who join your firm as a result of your great employer brand are more likely to be engaged. Better employee engagement leads to better productivity, job satisfaction, and lower turnover rates.

Neglecting to incorporate employer branding into your strategic talent management initiatives is a risk, as it could result in your best talent being lured away by your competitors. In today's competitive job market, investing in employer branding is not just beneficial, it's essential for talent retention and organizational success.

4. RETURN TO THE OFFICE IMMEDIATELY OR I'M FIRED? REALLY?

There is plenty to be written about the benefits of remote work for organizations, but what about the benefits of remote work for employees? However, keep in mind that some jobs just cannot be done remotely.

A CEO recently told me, "I am about to put a stop to this work-from-home thing." Curious, because the statement came as a surprise. "You just know people aren't working when they are remote. The other day, someone told my admin that they had just returned from walking their dog," he explained. "If the employee was working in the office and left over their break to walk their dog or run an errand, would that make them any more or less pro-ductive than a remote employee?" I questioned the CEO.

I felt compelled to confront the implication of 'slacking,' given that my colleague's firm had seen record profits and sales during the previous two years, during which time every single employee worked from home. An organiza-tion's leadership that suddenly doesn't trust employees to be productive unless they're visually and physically ac-counted for has many more difficulties that might po-tentially affect profitability, least of all a remote employee who goes for a stroll with their dog.

In early 2020, the world was confronted with a pandemic that forced workplaces to swiftly adapt their operations to prioritize safety and well-being. Governments issued "shelter in place" orders, restricting people from leaving their homes except for essential reasons. Non-essential businesses shuttered, leaving employees to navigate ill-ness, reduced work hours, school closures, and quaran-tine measures.

Amid these unprecedented challenges, organizations learned valuable lessons about flexibility and adaptation. It became evident that there are multiple ways to work, conduct business, and connect in an increasingly digital world. Notably, organizations discovered that the pro-ductivity of their employees often thrived in remote work settings. A study conducted by Stanford University over nine months highlighted several factors contributing to this increased productivity, including fewer workplace distractions, improved working conditions, and reduced sick leave. Moreover, the study found that remote work led to higher job satisfaction and a significant 50% decrease in attrition rates within organizations.

Remote work undeniably offers a multitude of benefits to employees, beyond just increased productivity. These advantages have become particularly apparent during the ongoing pandemic, which continues to affect work patterns for many despite significant vaccination efforts. Here are some notable benefits:

➢ Remote work often leads to higher job satisfaction as employees gain better control over managing competing priorities, a challenge that the pandemic exacerbated.

➢ When it comes to health and well-being, studies show that remote work can help reduce physical fatigue caused by long commutes, particularly during times of high fuel prices. Additionally, recent studies consistently report that remote workers are more productive than in-office workers, spending less time on unproductive tasks and achieving a 47% boost in productivity.

➢ Given these benefits, it's important to question why remote work is sometimes viewed negatively. Many organizations are still adapting to the reality that most non-essential workers will continue to work remotely. It's crucial to treat employees who have contributed significantly to businesses during the pandemic with consideration, rather than mandating that they resign.

➢ However, it's important to recognize that remote work isn't suitable for everyone. Some employees prefer the normalcy of in-office work, and there are concerns about isolation, lack of routine, technical challenges, and loss of company culture associated with remote work.

➢ Isolation can be a significant issue for some remote workers, who may miss the social interactions and camaraderie of an office. Remote work can also blur the boundaries between work and personal life, leading to overwork and burnout. While working from home can be flexible, it requires self-discipline to ensure a healthy work-life balance.

➢ Technical challenges can also arise, as not all employees have access to the necessary technology and infrastructure for effective remote work. Additionally, remote work can diminish the sense of belonging to a company's culture and mission, despite the use of video conferencing to facilitate team communication.

➢ While remote work offers many benefits, it's important to consider individual preferences and concerns when deciding on the best work arrangement. Gestures, and speech intonation all contribute to a fruitful collaboration experience.

➢ Mental Health: Isolation, lack of social interaction, and the challenges of remote work can take a toll on employees' mental health.

The most convenient approach is to become a hybrid model. But it is never that simple.

Keep in mind that some jobs just cannot be completed remotely. It's not fair nor unjust, it's simply the way things are. Identify alternative methods to engage important personnel who are unable to work remotely.

Discovering alternative methods of work is becoming a main goal for some firms, and adjusting to working from home requires deeper thought than alternatives or real estate and should engage the people most impacted – the employees.

5. MANAGING POLITICAL DISCUSSIONS IN THE WORKPLACE

Political discussions have taken center stage in various parts of the world, including the UK and Brazil, and they have inevitably seeped into our daily lives, even permeating our workplaces. While these conversations can be intellectually stimulating and thought-provoking, they can quickly take a turn for the uncomfortable. The fine line between the right to free speech and creating a hostile work environment is not always clear-cut; it can be elusive.

As an HR leader, I found myself grappling with the dilemma of whether to intervene in a particularly intense political discussion unfolding in the breakroom. I hesitated because the boundary between safeguarding freedom of speech and preventing a hostile work environment was far from obvious. I decided to observe and hope for the best.

The National Labor Relations Act explicitly prohibits employers from restricting employees' discussions about the terms of their employment. Much of the spirited discussion I witnessed pertained directly to income, taxes, and other employment-related matters, although it may have ventured into more unrelated topics like totalitarianism. In this delicate situation, I couldn't help but wonder if I was inadvertently inviting a complaint related to a hostile work environment. The answer, perhaps, was not entirely clear.

While government and certain municipal employees have some protections under the First Amendment's free speech rights, freedom of speech is not protected in most US private companies unless your employees work in one of the few states where political affiliation is considered a protected class. While a conversation about political diversity among employees may be beneficial and educational, when does it become a liability, and how can it be controlled and assessed against one's constitutional right to free speech? Whether your employees' favorite political hero is red, white, black, or orange, here are some pointers for keeping a unified, safe, and productive work environment for everybody as we approach yet another politically sensitive period:

Promote a culture of respect from the top down

Regardless of whether an employee holds a high-ranking position in the C-suite or occupies a more modest role at the reception desk, it's important to acknowledge that everyone possesses their own beliefs and values, which are deeply personal and significant.

Promote an atmosphere that fosters respectful and open exchanges of these beliefs, free from any apprehension or intimidation. Creating an environment where employees feel secure in sharing their perspectives without the fear of facing negative consequences encourages vital conversations. Such discussions are instrumental in cultivating an inclusive culture within your organization, where diverse viewpoints are valued and embraced.

Proceed with caution

It's crucial to have a deep understanding of your organizational culture and recognize when political discussions might carry risks. In some instances, an employee who receives disciplinary action for their performance or behavior may link this consequence to an unrelated comment or opinion they previously shared during a heated political debate.

While encouraging open dialogue can be a positive step toward engagement, it's equally important to remember that the manner in which you express your viewpoints can be just as significant, if not more so, than the content of your message. This consideration is essential for maintaining a harmonious workplace where diverse opinions are respected while minimizing potential misunderstandings or conflicts.

Know when enough is enough

In an environment that promotes respectful debate, it's essential to remind employees to be aware of social cues and recognize when their colleagues might be feeling uncomfortable. As a leader, do not hesitate to step in and redirect any discussion that starts to become aggressive, disrespectful, or threatening in any way.

Maintaining a healthy and constructive atmosphere for discussions means not only fostering open dialogue but also ensuring that it remains respectful and considerate of others' feelings and perspectives. Leaders play a pivotal role in upholding these standards and guiding conversations back to a productive and respectful path when needed.

Review your policies for consistency

During election periods, it's important to reinforce your organization's policies related to electronic communications, harassment, cultural sensitivity, and even dress code. While individuals have the right to express their political beliefs, it's crucial to maintain a workplace environment that is respectful and inclusive.

For instance, clothing items or accessories with political slogans, such as "Make America Great Again" or "Swing Left," may be considered a form of self-expression by some employees. However, it's essential to be aware that such attire can send various messages to your customers and co-workers, some of whom may prefer fashion that is more neutral and not politically charged. Encourage employees to be mindful of the impact of their clothing choices on the workplace environment and overall professionalism.

Remember your role as an employer

As an employer, it is your responsibility to ensure a safe and comfortable work environment for all employees. While the First Amendment protects individuals' rights to free speech, it does not exempt employers from establishing guidelines and boundaries regarding political discussions in the workplace. It is essential to create a productive and respectful atmosphere that promotes inclusivity and sensitivity.

Political discussions in the workplace can be constructive when conducted with respect, inclusiveness, and sensitivity. These qualities are the hallmarks of a progressive organization that values diverse perspectives and encourages open dialogue. However, it's crucial to strike a balance and manage such discussions to prevent disruptions that may impede your organization's progress or create a hostile work environment.

6. THE BENEFITS OF EMPLOYEE BENEFITS

It's that time of year again, with a crispness in the air that hints at the upcoming winter. This season brings thoughts of hot apple cider, cozy fireplaces, football, and one of HR's most significant events, Open Enrollment. While it might not quite match the excitement of the Super Bowl, employee benefits are a crucial aspect of an employee's experience, often influencing their engagement, loyalty, tenure, and overall job satisfaction.

Employees frequently have a wish list of extra benefits in addition to the essential core benefits normally supplied at the outset of work, such as life insurance, long and short-term disability coverage, and retirement plans. Medical, dental, and vision care, Flexible Spending Accounts (FSAs), Employee Aid Programs (EAPs), and other benefits like relocation aid and tuition reimbursement may be included. Employers who do not offer a complete benefits package may find it difficult to recruit and retain top-tier individuals. To remain competitive, it is critical to offer perks that go beyond the fundamentals.

The law requires employers to provide employees with certain benefits. You must:

- Provide time off to vote or serve a jury
- Provide time off for military service
- Pay state and federal unemployment taxes
- Comply with compensation requirements
- Comply with the Family Medical Leave Act
- Contribute to State short-term disability
- Withhold FICA taxes and pay your own portion of FICA taxes,

How to build engagement using benefits:

➢ **Appeal to the employee you want to attract and retain**

Consider the perks that will make your benefits package stand out when compared to your competitors if you want to attract and retain the sort of talent you need to take your business to the next level. When it comes to health and well-being, studies show that remote work can help reduce physical fatigue caused by long commutes, particularly during times of high fuel prices. Additionally, recent studies consistently report that remote workers are more productive than in-office workers, spending less time on unproductive tasks and achieving a 47% boost in productivity.

Given these benefits, it's important to question why remote work is sometimes viewed negatively. Many organizations are still adapting to the reality that most non-essential workers will continue to work remotely. It's crucial to treat employees who have contributed significantly to businesses during the pandemic with consideration, rather than mandating that they resign.

However, it's important to recognize that remote work isn't suitable for everyone. Some employees prefer the normalcy of in-office work, and there are concerns about isolation, lack of routine, technical challenges, and loss of company culture associated with remote work.

Isolation can be a significant issue for some remote workers, who may miss the social interactions and camaraderie of an office. Remote work can also blur the boundaries between work and personal life, leading to overwork and burnout. While working from home can be flexible, it requires self-discipline to ensure a healthy work-life balance.

Technical challenges can also arise, as not all employees have access to the necessary technology and infrastructure for effective remote work. Additionally, remote work can diminish the sense of belonging to a company's culture and mission, despite the use of video conferencing to facilitate team communication.

While remote work offers many benefits, it's important to consider individual preferences and concerns when deciding on the best work arrangement, consider going beyond the essentials, and try providing employees advantages that are appealing to your employee base, such as substantial PTO accrual, tuition reimbursement, or a retirement plan, to make your company more appealing.

> **Promote loyalties and engagement**
Building a loyal and engaged staff requires the correct benefits package. The more concerns that a complete, strong benefits package can eliminate, the more your workers can focus on their company objectives. Employees do not want to be concerned about their medical care, pensions, or income if they are unable to work. They want the assurance that they are "covered," that they have what they need when they need it, and that they have the peace of mind to perform their best job. When you invest in benefits, you are also investing in your workers.

> **Job satisfaction**
Your colleagues are more likely to repay the effort and take their jobs more seriously if you understand and respond to their demands. The simplest technique to boost employee job happiness is to demonstrate your concern for them. Survey your employees on what advantages or perks are essential to them regularly and be prepared to take action. Engage your workers in benefit choices that affect them and let them know their input is valued.

> ➤ **A comprehensive benefits package can be profitable**
> Offering a well-rounded benefit package benefits both the employee and the company by allowing for a reduced pay base match for state and federal unemployment taxes. A lower pay base match is never a convincing argument for choosing a benefits package.

In conclusion

Investing in your employees through benefits can be not only profitable but also highly productive. Benefits are deeply connected to your employees' well-being, addressing their health, welfare, and retirement needs. It's crucial not to overlook the potential to use these benefits to make a positive impact on your organization as a whole.

CHAPTER 3

Diversity

YESCENE

"You're more than qualified but unfortunately we already
have a black woman working here"

1. WHAT YOU WON'T HEAR AT THE DIVERSITY TASK FORCE MEETING

Diversity, inclusion, and equity extend far deeper than
rhetoric. We engage in safe, polite discussions about making our workplace environments more diverse, inclusive,
and equitable, valuing differences, and welcoming everyone, regardless of those differences. We've all heard the
usual conversation.

However, lost in the politically correct tone of the meeting are the deep undertones of racism, sexism, antisemitism, and implicit and explicit bias that have been woven into the fabric of our workplace culture. So much so, that it has left some of us feeling like we exist in an alternative universe every day of our working lives. We are the individuals at your company willing to lead initiatives to attract and retain a diverse pool of candidates and employees, advocating for more career opportunities, to impact the environment and drive change. But we rarely talk about some of the experiences that leave us with a healthy amount of skepticism that things are likely to change unless there's a cultural reset of sorts.

We are realistic about how deeply ingrained the issues are that hinder organic inclusion and acceptance. We know that diversity, inclusion, and equity remain a heavy lift. While we may appear socially well-adjusted, adaptable within the spaces we inhabit, and capable of moving comfortably in many political circles within the workplace, the truth is that not a day goes by without a reminder that our presence and acceptance are marginal at best, as you'll soon read. We are resilient, if not numb, and skilled at keeping potential threats in front of us. We rely on self-affirmation and are constantly aware of our surroundings, even when they've been deemed "safe." We come with a series of experiences and short stories spanning our careers that have left our rose-colored glasses crystal clear and untainted when it comes to all things related to diversity. These are just a few of the experiences I've encountered in the fairly recent past. I have:

➢ unwittingly received an interoffice envelope from an admin containing blackface pictures of my colleagues, obviously taken after I had left a work function that I had organized. It was clear that this was not meant for my consumption.

➢ attended a game between the Warriors and the Clippers in suite seats next to my boss, whom I also considered my "friend." During the game, my boss jumped to his feet and screamed out "F*&#ing monkey!" at one of the Black home team players for missing a shot.

➢ been denied a promotion with the explanation that "this role will be responsible for consulting and persuading CFOs and C-Suite executives, and they typically are more comfortable taking advice from people that mirror their demographic."

➢ had my new boss say to me, "I'm here to support you. If there is something you don't understand, don't feel bad. I know that sometimes African Americans have cognitive challenges. Don't ever be afraid to come to me; you'll never be punished for asking questions." This happened when I was in a senior role.

➤ inquired why the relocation package I was offered was significantly less than others in my role had received when transferring internally. A candid HR Generalist told me, "Well, we have what I call the diversity relocation package that I have been instructed to offer to people of color, and then we have the standard relocation package that I have been told to offer everyone else. But now that you have asked, I have been told I am obligated to offer it to you as well.

➤ been chased around my desk (literally) by a C-suite executive with a fascination for "Black men with rich dark skin" who routinely asked invasive questions like, "Is it Black all over? Can I see your bare back...?"

➤ received feedback in a performance appraisal that I sometimes have a "flat affect" and was advised to smile more because "you're dark-skinned, and you can come across as threatening and menacing, which can make people uncomfortable. People like it when you smile anyway."

➤ overheard a colleague assume that I was married to a white woman based on the assumption that my wife was super nice, had her own business, and was super stylish.

➤ been offered the role as the head of Diversity and Inclusion but was told that my primary duties would involve organizing potlucks and cultural crafts days, with an implied lack of significance to the role.

➢ as the HR Manager of a facility predominantly employing young white females, had an executive ask me, "As a Black guy, how can you stand the temptation? For you, this must be like being a fox in a henhouse."

➢ faced questions from colleagues, such as, "Did you receive your private school education abroad through some sort of disadvantaged youth program?" and "Who paid for that?"

➢ consistently got called by the names of two other Black men working in the building, one being ten years older, a foot shorter, and significantly lighter in weight with snow-white hair, and the other being nearly a foot taller, fifteen years younger, and built like a bodybuilder.

➢ consistently received significantly lower pay than my white counterparts for performing the same work. This has become so commonplace that I no longer consider it a disparity; it's just how it is.

So, don't be misled: we have a lot of work to do in terms of Diversity, Inclusion, and Equity. Take time to comprehend everyone's experience as you develop your strategy to address this newfound social consciousness, so you know where to start.

2. IF IT'S "UNCONSCIOUS" BIAS, THAT'S BETTER, RIGHT?

If Nostradamus had predicted the state of equality in the year 2021, he would likely have predicted equality for all human beings. Yet here we are, in 2021, still struggling with, of all things, INEQUALITY. Let's be honest; the workplace can be a hotspot for biases and discrimination that provide inequality with its foundation, starting with the hiring process.

We are all human. We can all agree on that much, I think. As humans, we tend to make decisions heuristically, or by making cognitive shortcuts as we have been programmed to do. However, some situations require a more analytical and objective approach. Relying solely on instinct or the rule of thumb can show up as implicit bias if we are not cognizant or thoughtful about our hiring and screening practices.

Unconscious biases are unconscious attitudes and stereotypes that manifest in our workplace, particularly in the recruiting and hiring process. These biases operate outside of our awareness and can be in direct contradiction to our most tightly held beliefs, and often will show up in our affect or behavior toward another individual. Freeing ourselves of unconscious bias and making hiring decisions based on them is easier said than done because often we are unaware that they exist and therefore may not realize the impact these biases have on hiring outcomes for the organization and the candidates themselves. When it comes to health and well-being, studies show that remote work can help reduce physical fatigue caused by long commutes, particularly during times of high fuel prices. Additionally, recent studies consistently report that remote workers are more productive than in-office workers, spending less time on unproductive tasks and achieving a 47% boost in productivity.

Given these benefits, it's important to question why remote work is sometimes viewed negatively. Many organizations are still adapting to the reality that most non-essential workers will continue to work remotely. It's crucial to treat employees who have contributed significantly to businesses during the pandemic with consideration, rather than mandating that they resign.

However, it's important to recognize that remote work isn't suitable for everyone. Some employees prefer the normalcy of in-office work, and there are concerns about isolation, lack of routine, technical challenges, and loss of company culture associated with remote work.

Isolation can be a significant issue for some remote workers, who may miss the social interactions and camaraderie of an office. Remote work can also blur the boundaries between work and personal life, leading to overwork and burnout. While working from home can be flexible, it requires self-discipline to ensure a healthy work-life balance.

Technical challenges can also arise, as not all employees have access to the necessary technology and infrastructure for effective remote work. Additionally, remote work can diminish the sense of belonging to a company's culture and mission, despite the use of video conferencing to facilitate team communication.

While remote work offers many benefits, it's important to consider individual preferences and concerns when deciding on the best work arrangement.

The first step toward mitigating unconscious biases is to define and accept their reality. Unfortunately, there are so many different forms of implicit biases that this page cannot adequately identify them all. But, just in case you believe you've heard it all, I'll share a few recent incidents with you.

> **Case # 01**

Bias, (there is such a thing), often targets Black people, specifically those with afro-textured hair that hasn't been chemically straightened. Afro-textured hair has frequently been seen as unprofessional, unattractive, and unclean.

The organization conducted a national search and found a candidate from Atlanta. She was highly qualified and educated and nailed her phone screen. By all accounts, we'd found our next VP of Finance. However, the offer was extended to the second runner-up, a lesser qualified candidate. I asked the recruiter to explain why. His response was, "They (the hiring panel) liked her, but she had those things in her hair, and some of them felt her hairdo didn't embody the brand."

So, I went to the hiring manager (who was also the CFO) for more information. He agreed that she was by far the most qualified on paper but said, "I just couldn't get past the whole hair thing."

➢ **Case # 02**

Racial Bias, a form of implicit bias, refers to attitudes or stereotypes that affect an individual's understanding, actions, and decisions unconsciously.

The candidate came with a master's in finance and a successful history in operations for a healthcare system three times the size of our own. He was by far the most qualified of the four finalists from a pool of 80. He was personable, innovative, had lots of great ideas, and according to the recruiter, "could elevate the team."

So, when I saw the third-choice candidate sitting in new hire orientation, I asked the recruiter what happened to this candidate everyone was excited about it. Her response was, "Everyone loved him, and they thought he was great, but some people thought the staff might be a little intimidated."

So, I went to the hiring manager to check on the matter. I was told that they "loved" the candidate but there was some concern that a guy of his size and stature (6'7 tall, 300 lbs. or so) might be a bit intimidating to the predominantly white millennial team. I could see the staff being scared (expletive) by this big, intense-looking Black guy in their one-on-ones (raucous laughter).

➤ **Case # 03**

The Horn Effect is a bias that surfaces when something negative about the candidate grabs our attention and we can't move beyond it. It could be a character flaw, an aspect of their personality, or even the sound of their voice that drives your decision not to hire them.

The frontrunner was a highly qualified Asian woman. She came prepared, with great responses, knowledgeable, engaging, and met or exceeded every qualification. When the panel passed on the candidate after less than an hour of interviewing her, I followed up with the hiring manager who responded, "We were turned off by her voice; she had to let us know that her boyfriend chartered a private jet to whisk her away to a romantic island for her birthday, AND she was wearing a diamond-encrusted watch an interview and carrying a Gucci bag! It was just one thing after the other with that one, and that voice, ugh! We're not about all of that here, but super qualified." So, they went with the second-choice candidate. Her tenure was brief.

So, what can you do about hiring bias?

- Ensure that recruiters and hiring managers have had interview training that addresses typical hiring biases.
- Use standardized interview instructions to ensure consistency.
- Make employment decisions based on evidence rather than preconceptions.

Consider including a blind resume screening in your process and ensure that your interview panels are diverse. Most importantly, make it a practice to debrief often with your team and recruiting manager, and be prepared to call out any actual or apparent unconscious biases.

3. DISCRIMINATION: A HAIRY SITUATION

Last month, the New York City Commission on Human Rights banned discrimination based on hair. My elation that society had chipped away another chunk of the granite mountain that is discrimination immediately turned to shame, as I was left wondering why such a law was necessary in the year 2019 in the first place. This took me back to a time when I was on the interview loop for a senior executive position. The candidate was a delightful, Ivy League-educated Black woman from South Carolina. She was smart, friendly, and the frontrunner for this role. Weeks passed, and I found out that another candidate who was identified during the interview process as "not having all of the skills that we desired" had been selected for the role. I asked the recruiter why, and I was told that the feedback on the Black woman was, "She did not embody our brand," wink, wink. No, she winked.

More specifically, the recruiter told me that a small minority of the interview loop took offense to the woman's short locs and felt that although she was by far the superior candidate, her natural locs would not befit an executive at our organization. So they went with the lesser candidate, who, by then, had already been terminated for quite literally assaulting a subordinate. In hindsight, perhaps a blonde pixie hairdo was not an indicator of competence.

In another instance, I had managers express concern that a young Black employee's substantial natural afro could put our healthcare facility at risk for lice. They were demanding that I order him to cut his hair. I was dumbfounded that an afro held that much power; never mind there had been two lice infestations before him being employed with the facility, and we had a young Caucasian employee with an equally large (un-natural) afro who was employed there at the time of both previous infestations. For some reason, he was never considered a culprit, just cute with "funky hair." There was no conclusive evidence in all hair history that would support the assertion that a natural or unnatural afro was a hotbed for lice or had toppled an organization. I sported a big puffy afro for all of my childhood and most of my young adult life, and I am happy to report that I am 57 years lice-free. Aside from the sheer absurdity of these incidents, there was a sadness that career opportunities could be compromised because of hair.

As far back as 1866, federal, state, and even local governments found the need to create protections against discrimination for individuals that belong to specific groups, known today as protected classes. Protected classes aim to prevent employers (among other entities) from discriminating against candidates and employees based on sex, race, color, religion, creed, national origin, sexual orientation, gender identity and gender expression, disability, genetic information, and in some areas, political affiliation. Hair has not made the list of protected classes, but the mere fact there is some level of legislation banning discrimination because of it is telling. Even though my afro has long since betrayed me, protected classes, afros, locs, and braids aside, I live for the day when we won't need laws to keep our biases in check. Those of us with the power to influence the candidate experience, impact a career, drive engagement, and create and foster an environment of inclusiveness, have the added responsibility of being thought partners when it comes to challenging norms and conventions.

Why does a hairstyle provoke such judgment?

What constitutes normal hair, and why? Take an honest self-assessment of your instant visceral reaction the next time you see an employee, applicant, or business partner with unusual hair, no matter how uncomfortable you feel doing so.

4. CULTIVATING DIVERSITY: A LONG-TERM INVESTMENT STRATEGY

Mismanaging cultural diversity in the workplace causes unhealthy tensions and a loss of team productivity. Your company is exponentially stronger when you foster an atmosphere of acceptance. While recently reminiscing about my time with a previous employer, I am reminded of a time when, within two weeks, one employee told another she looked like Aunt Jemima, another engaged colleague in a debate that Black people were genetically unable to swim, and yet another employee said to her colleague, a Stanford graduate, "by now you've been in America long enough to be speaking English without an accent, weird." We could always blame Mercury being in retrograde and leave it at that OR these incidents could have been a call to action for some cultural sensitivity, or is it cultural competency training?

Developing both cultural sensitivity and cultural competency results in an ability to understand, communicate with, and effectively interact with people across cultures. It helps us work more collaboratively with varying cultural beliefs and values without assigning judgment, good, bad, right, or wrong. To invest in creating a culturally sensitive and culturally competent workplace means making a cultural shift from checking the box to skill-building, and the development of these skills is well worth the investment.

The U.S. Bureau of Census projects that by 2050, the U.S. population will reach over 400 million, about 47% larger than in the year 2000, with primary ethnic minority groups, specifically Hispanics, Black people, Asian-Americans, and Native Americans, constituting almost 50% of the population in 2050. About 57% of the population under the age of 18 and 34% over the age of 65 will be in the ethnic minority. There are 32 different cultural groups with unique ethnic or national identities, religions, and histories, just within the group of Asian Americans and Pacific Islanders alone.

We can no longer afford to view cultural diversity among our employees as something to be discussed only in hushed tones. It's not something to be ignored or brushed aside. I once referred to myself as Black, only to be corrected by a white colleague with, "Can you use 'African American'? 'Black' is so negative." Did he not consider that not all Black people are African American? Perhaps I am Cuban, Brazilian, Panamanian, or African, and not American at all. Have we truly progressed to accepting one another's differences, or are we working overtime to make those differences invisible?

The more different people's experiences and backgrounds are, the more diverse their viewpoints and opinions become. A culturally diverse brainstorming session can be a prime environment for outside-the-box thinking. Your team will then be better equipped to develop fresh ideas that meet the needs of the diverse marketplace we work in. You can also broaden your service range, as cultural diversity includes inviting a variety of on-the-job skills that drive innovation in your company and reflect the world around you. Creating an atmosphere of mutual understanding and respect lays a firm foundation for building effective teams.

5. SOCIAL INJUSTICE AND THE WORKPLACE: A CALL TO ACTION

You may have noticed that there is a spirit of "woke" consciousness in the air within your organization. Your employees, shareholders, and industry collectives are coming together to make their desires for social and cultural change heard. Let's face it, the dawn of a new era is upon us. Gone are the days when topics like racial equality, social justice, white privilege, and an ongoing epidemic of Black men and women being killed in the streets are relegated to discussions far from the employee break room and even further from the C-Suites. This social justice movement is gaining traction, and if that scares you, it's not a good sign.

In the past 12-18 months, we've seen women walking out in protest of the mishandling of sexual misconduct claims, employees using their shares to get the attention of the board over concerns about the lack of action on climate change, protests over facial recognition software further marginalizing people of color and immigrants, and that's just within the corporate world. Some might say we are watching America transform before our very eyes into a totalitarian society akin to the fictional Republic of Gilead from Margaret Atwood's novel "The Handmaid's Tale." More people are fully realizing that there is very little diversity in executive-level positions – or anywhere else, for that matter. There is a new kind of industry organizing around uncomfortable social issues. It has arrived quickly and – potentially – with a high personal cost to your organization.

Is your organization prepared for change?

The good news (for some) is that, by all accounts, this movement is only going to grow in support; and more inclusive and fair-minded employees are mobilizing and strategizing ways of holding businesses and their leaders accountable. The bad news (for others) is that the system has worked as it was designed to during a time when Jim Crow reigned supreme, and women were called housewives. That's a lot of social structure to tear down. Change is overdue, and your organization may not be prepared to manage it correctly.

How an organization responds to this new movement depends on the ability of leadership to see the organization through the lens of employees at all levels and to take accountability for the culture they have fostered. While an organization may be rightfully committed to the inclusion of all things LGBTQ and pay equity for women, there may be little evidence to the naked eye that "Black Lives Matter." This cannot be a one-size-fits-all type of change. It needs to be done intentionally and with multiple perspectives involved. (Tip: Should you choose to beef up your Diversity and Inclusion and/or Social Justice initiatives as a result of the recent worldwide call to action, please refrain from starting your campaign with a declaration that "All Lives Matter"). This movement is also not going anywhere anytime soon. With the Global Climate Strike kicking off, continued Black Lives Matter protests taking over many cities, and an American presidential election just months away – it may be just starting to gain traction. The question is, how prepared are you to listen, learn, and take action? The methods of yesteryear (or even last year) aren't likely to work anymore.

What's different about this social injustice movement?

Millennial and Generation Z employees are on the rise, and they are more concerned about the employer brand they represent vs. their interests. They are concerned about the footprint and social values of the organization they work for. They also expect that the businesses they buy from think of and make a meaningful contribution to people, communities, and society — not just profits. Inherently shifting the nature of recruitment and consumer demand, the values held by this more socially committed demographic have already managed to infiltrate and influence more conservative organizations, including those headed by leadership teams indifferent to the wants, needs, and desires of diverse employees that have been marginalized in the past.

We are living in a time where racism, anti-Semitism, gender bias, cultural polarization, and even modern-day lynching are being woven into the fabric of our daily experience, for some more than others. Don't miss and foster more progressive environments. Some will choose to do nothing while others rise to the occasion. If you are ready to be part of a progressive movement for social change and impactful diversity and equality, we will be providing some best practices to support you in this opportunity to take a stand and lead change. All organizations will face challenges in determining how best to respond to the call to eradicate injustice journey.

6. IT'S TIME FOR MEANINGFUL ACTION ON EQUITY AND INCLUSION

So here we are, in the middle of the most significant social movement since the 1960s. Employees are asking for your organization's commitment to social change, and the only response they have heard is the sound of crickets. But you have cultural sensitivity and awareness training modules in your LMS, a mission statement that includes the words "Diversity and Inclusion," and you might even have a policy that provides for the term "Zero Tolerance" (if you're cutting-edge progressive). What more do these employees want from you?

Employees want to know that combating racial discrimination within your organization is essential. Symbolic gestures of fairness and racial equality are no longer an acceptable form of resolution to the ongoing covert forms of daily discrimination prevalent within the workplace. Now, more than ever, employees, customers, and even communities are looking to your brand to see how you are responding to antiquated, ridiculous notions that any race is actually "supreme" or has "power" over another. They want to know what action is being taken to promote equality and social justice… you're on the watch list.

First steps to fostering equity, inclusion, and anti-racism

It's time for organizations to do the work – to create programs that foster growth along racial lines and inclusion for all employees. If you are unable to create a separate department dedicated to diversity and inclusion within your organization, consider a collaboration between Human Resources, Training and Development, Communications, Legal, and your IT Department. Collectively, such a team can establish goals for hiring, career pathing, conducting compensation reviews for pay equity adjustments, programs for ongoing cultural awareness training beyond new hire orientation, tracking and measuring outcomes, and embedding equity, inclusion, and anti-racism into your values, training, and culture.

Gone are the days of simply checking the box by declaring Affirmative Action. You may feel that a conversation about one's thoughts and experiences doesn't belong in the workplace, but now is the time to make these issues real and personal. Not sure where to begin? Consider the following suggestions as you begin your initiatives:

How to launch a meaningful initiative for social change

You must keep the conversation alive. This is a turning point not only in the workplace but also in the world. The first step is acknowledging the injustices that exist and expressing your commitment to the global initiative to do better.

The next steps should include initiating meaningful, honest discussions, forming employee affinity groups, and creating a safe space for everyone to dialogue about race. Most importantly, seek input from missing voices to help obtain different ideas on how to promote an inclusive workplace at all levels.

Just be real

Be honest about the lack of diversity among your employees and how it has impacted your organization. Stop acting like you haven't noticed. We all see it, some of us more clearly than others. There is nothing like realizing that ascending the ranks may be a struggle because nobody on the leadership team looks like you. One of the advantages of the white privilege that people wear like a badge of honor is not having to think about it. You may be surprised at how one can be impacted when they don't see themselves in the "portrait" of an organization. Some organizations unintentionally perpetuate racism by failing to acknowledge issues within their own culture. This may be a good time to ask someone how they are impacted. As uncomfortable as this conversation may be – have it! You will set yourself up for a progressively better and more productive dialogue with each successive conversation.

Make a public commitment to diversity and the eradication of unconscious bias. The hiring process is just one of many ways employers can combat racial discrimination. Leaders are the ones who establish the company culture whether it's intentional or not. Taking meaningful action against racism means leaders need to step up and support Talent Acquisition initiatives aimed at mitigating unconscious bias. The Harvard Business School Working Knowledge blog published an article discussing research findings that minority job applicants are omitting references to their race on their resumes in hopes of improving their odds of getting a job. The article explained how "Asian applicants often change their names to something more American sounding" as well as Americanizing their interests by using common white Western cultural activities such as snowboarding or hiking. African Americans will hide their involvement in Black organizations by removing the word "black" from a professional society or scholarship. They do so because it has proven to get them more interviews. It's time to acknowledge that unconscious bias is hardwired into our processes and a significant commitment is required to make meaningful change.

Organizations have a responsibility to shout from the mountaintop a commitment to diversity and the value it brings to the company, as well as actively communicating their stance on racial discrimination and equity in the workplace. A stronger, healthier workplace culture is dependent on having core values that address equity, inclusion, and anti-racism, as well as ensuring those values are integrated into every policy, decision, and process. Want to truly make a difference? Go beyond that to actively denounce any policies, behaviors, and practices that contradict your core values, thereby making it impossible for racism of any sort to thrive.

7. THE IMPACT OF CULTIVATING DIVERSITY

What do a Vampire, Burlesque Performer, Professional Hugger, Showgirl, and Civil War Union Soldier who fights faithfully in the battle at Gettysburg every year all have in common? They could all have day jobs in your organization.

Diversity in the workplace – what does it look like?

The above diverse, wonderful people are all real. A not-so-nefarious, self-proclaimed vampire with fang implants needed an accommodation to work from home on sunny days, due to a legitimate photo-sensitivity abnormality. Another employee who danced burlesque part-time needed help managing an identity crisis when she wanted to be referred to in all records and communications as Bettie (as in Bettie Page) when her legal name was Jill. The professional hugger was a determined gentleman who insisted that the company tuition reimbursement policy applied to his professional hugging course using the argument that what he was learning from his hugging courses could be applied to his current role as a Financial Analyst.

Other real-life examples of amazing diversity include an East Indian Hindu HR Generalist who was a converted Southern Baptist... A Black Jewish woman from Detroit who spoke Hebrew fluently and was a successful consultant... A Buddhist Monk, who was also a Kung Fu expert and the organization's most talented labor attorney... A reformed White Supremacist, who was among the first to the altar once same-sex marriage became legalized in California (they made a lovely bi-racial couple). Each of these individuals was a stellar employee who excelled remarkably in their respective disciplines, and they all brought a uniquely delightful interest to the environment and their work.

Diversity goes far deeper than the color of an employee's skin, hair color, or race. It also has to do with a variety of characteristics, including, but not limited to religion, sexual orientation, and ethnicity. Diversity encompasses interest, personality, age, hobbies, ideals, values, talents, and even cognitive styles. It is something to be recognized, promoted as a valued asset, and something to be capitalized on. Diversity is not a chore; it's a goal and your organization is exponentially stronger when you foster and promote it.

The benefits of diversity and inclusiveness

An organization that is represented by a variety of cultures, perspectives, ideas, and skill sets is an organization with a strategic advantage. Diversity brings to any organization a multi-dimensional edge in an evolving global marketplace. You may find that diversity provides an opportunity for employees to enjoy and learn from one another's differences which promotes mutual respect and tolerance, and that a diversity of perspectives and ideas gives rise to creative solutions and innovative ways to execute and deliver to both your internal and external stakeholders. Some organizations still view diversity as a requirement vs. an aspiration. Consider it an investment in your employees and the future of your organization. Successful organizations have made diversity and inclusion a critical business imperative.

How does your organization measure up?

If your goal is to foster an environment of diversity and inclusiveness consider starting the process with a preliminary assessment of your organization's commitment to the cause as follows:

☐ Do you have a current set of diversity policies?

☐ Do you have any quantifiable diversity practices?

☐ Is diversity and inclusion a part of your corporate Social Responsibility Statement?

☐ What were the results of the diversity auditing the company has conducted?

☐ Has your organization conducted any briefings or training around the topic of diversity?

The following is a framework used to determine where an organization stands when it comes to attitude toward diversity. Where do you fall?

• Negative organization

• Has no equal opportunity policy in place

• Makes no claims to be an equal opportunities employer.

• Might not be complying with some equal opportunities laws

• Minimalist organization

- Makes claims to be of being an equal opportunities employer

- Has no written equal opportunity policy

- Has no procedures or diversity initiatives but reacts accordingly to any discrimination issues

- Compliant organization

- Has written an equal opportunity policy

- Has robust procedures in place to encourage diversity initiatives

- Proactive organization

- Actively creates diverse policies and strategies

- Monitors the outcome of initiatives to assess their success

- Consistently promotes equality using an established set of guidelines

Diversity is always worth the investment

The more diverse employee experiences and backgrounds are, the more diverse their viewpoints and opinions are. A strategic brainstorming session can be a prime environment where outside-the-box thinking can thrive. Your team will be better equipped to develop fresh ideas that will meet the needs of a diverse marketplace. You can also broaden your service range as cultural diversity includes inviting a variety of on-the-job skills that drive innovation in your company.

When you have a diverse workforce, diverse customers in your target market are more likely to trust your brand and feel comfortable doing business with your company. As our economy becomes increasingly global, your workforce will also become increasingly diverse. Your competitiveness and success will depend on your success in managing diversity and inclusion in your organization.

Make diversity a part of the overall talent management strategy. Aside from a positive impact on your bottom line, your employees' work experience will be enriched because of it. To invest in creating a diverse, collaborative, and inclusive workplace means making a cultural shift from checking the box to skill building, and the development of these skills is well worth the investment.

8. TRANSGENDERISM IN THE WORKPLACE: THE NEW NOT-SO-NEW NORMAL

Many years ago, I met a co-worker, Terry. Terry was quiet, but friendly enough, a bit of a loner, but social enough. Terry was introverted, but just outgoing enough to be someone to look forward to chatting with. We crossed paths frequently in the kitchen, the men's room, the elevator, Starbucks, etc. We would chat about everything from food, life, family, sports, and our love of shoes. One day, during a chat about our childhood, I came to know that the "guy" I knew as Terry was legally named Teresa, and Terry identified neither as he nor she, but as "transgender," something until then, I had never heard of before. And there began my indoctrination to being transgender.

The study of emotional intelligence demonstrates that we humans are pre-disposed to the judgment of others who are different. We cling to learned perspectives and behaviors and are quick to adopt established ideals of normalcy that are often one-dimensional. In today's workplace, HR leaders must be committed to creating an environment conducive to dialogue and honesty about the challenges of adopting a "new normal" and the challenges faced by trans employees that fit the very definition.

If your objective is to create a diverse inclusive workplace for ALL, you may find the following guidelines and policy changes useful:

Establish guidelines prohibiting gender bias

We are never as culturally fluent as we think we are. While we may be steeped in the nuances of our own particular environments and subcultures, never assume you are literate in others. Because myths and misconceptions can influence the behavior of co-workers toward individuals who identify as transgender, make sure your company provides training for all employees on gender-related issues in the workplace to ensure that co-workers do not intentionally or unintentionally create an environment that will negatively impact a transgender employee. Review your company handbook to make sure that it includes clear policies against discrimination and harassment, and the handbook needs to be distributed to employees with attestation of receipt. Most importantly, enforce the policy.

Refer to transgender employees by their preferred name

As they transition to their preferred gender identity, transgender employees may want to change their names. For example, an employee may change their name to a more common male or female name, or even an androgynous name, for example, from Teresa to Terry. While it may be challenging for co-workers to understand the change, HR can be instrumental in establishing an environment where transgender employees are addressed by whatever name and gender they prefer. When in conversation, co-workers should use pronouns that correspond to one's gender identity. Items such as office mailboxes and nameplates should also reflect the preferred name and gender pronouns.

Establishing clear bathroom designations

An inclusive workplace considers the needs of ALL employees. A transgender employee may be as sensitive to the use of single-sex bathrooms as their co-workers. Keep in mind that, sometimes, transgender employees may be transitioning toward their final gender identity. They may initially want to use a bathroom that corresponds to their biological sex but at some point, begin using restrooms that correspond to their new or anticipated gender identity. Wherever possible Human Resources should work with management to designate gender-neutral bathrooms that are available to ALL employees, not just transgender, male, or female.

Implement a gender-neutral employee dress code

Does your company have a dress code requirement that differs for men and women? For example, some employers may require male employees to wear pants while female employees are asked to wear skirts. The switch between pants and skirts may leave transitioning transgender employees feeling awkward and self-conscious. Human Resources can help by implementing a more gender-neutral dress code, not specifying gender-specific articles of clothing. Transgender employees may assume the appearance of their gender identity. Any dress codes and guidelines regarding the appearance of your employees that are consistent with business necessity should apply to transgender employees. However, employers should consider dress codes and guidelines that eliminate any sex stereotypes.

Address any discriminatory behavior and misconduct swiftly

Most importantly, Human Resources should address any misconduct that targets transgender employees in the same manner as other forms of discrimination. Your standard workplace investigatory protocols should be adhered to should there be accusations of gender bias. As always, the investigation should be properly documented and supported by any materials gathered during the investigation. In any organization, Human Resources is instrumental in building an innovative and creative environment, which will attract top talent and positively impact retention. A business that is inclusive and respectful of ALL its human capital is always good for business.

9. YOUR ORGANIZATION'S COMMITMENT TO LGBT PRIDE MONTH BEYOND JUST THE RAINBOW

Growing up, my parents shared many stories of the struggle, perseverance, and marginalization of Black people. My father frequently closed with, "There's no shame in being black, it just ain't easy at times." He wasn't kidding! I grew up in a society located smack dab in the middle of the land of the free, and home of the brave where what was consistently characterized as "normal" or "acceptable" looked very little like me. This made me even more committed to inclusiveness and promoting the ideal of freedom to be as we are and live unabashed and unapologetically–even when it's not easy. As an HR Leader, I am all for any opportunity to disrupt the notion that diversity is something to be hidden, downplayed, or stamped out. But this moment in time is not about me or mine; it's about our LGBT community, who like so many other groups, still face discrimination in employment for simply being who they are. This is an age-old struggle that began long before the Stonewall Riots of 1969. Here we are, three years after President Barack Obama proclaimed the month of June LGBT Pride Month, and HR Leaders have a prime opportunity, if not an obligation, to bring awareness to critical issues that relate to individuals who share our workplace. In my humble HR opinion, we tend to shy away from anything with the appearance of favoring one community of people over another when it comes to marginalized populations.

But let's look at it differently.

Try viewing your organization's response to LGBT Pride Month as the perfect opportunity to ensure that you are promoting inclusion and diversity in the workplace.

In his proclamation, President Obama called upon the people of the United States "to eliminate prejudice everywhere it exists, and to celebrate the great diversity of the American people." Who could have a problem with that? With that in mind, here are some ways to support your organization and employees during LGBT Pride Month.

Promote history

Even though this is LGBT Pride Month, there is nothing that says organizations can't take this opportunity to focus on some history 101. I had someone tell me the other day that Pride started in San Francisco when some guys got together to have a parade. "It was so successful it caught on." When I asked if the individual had heard of the Stonewall Riots, they asked if that was where the Watts Riots took place. Only days earlier I had someone ask, "Were your grandparents—or I guess it would be great grandparents—slaves?" Back in May, I had someone ask if, "Cinco de Mayo was the same thing as that Day of the Dead celebration thing."

I'm not trying to start anything—but sometimes we can be a little uninformed when it comes to history, particularly if it has not held a space of significance in our lives. Educate your employees on the historical significance of LGBT Pride. Share with your employees that this month was chosen in correlation with the Stonewall Riots, which occurred on June 28th, 1969, in New York City, and is considered by many the beginning of the modern LGBT rights movement. Sharing such history serves as a reminder to employers and employees of the major strides taken toward ensuring tolerance and diversity in the workplace today.

Conduct a culture check

Raise the question to your fellow leaders, "What is our stance on LGBT Pride Month?" If none is identified, this might be a good time to take one. This might be the perfect time to take a look at how your organization acknowledges LGBT Pride Month, Black History

Month, religious holidays/celebrations, Solstice, etc. Do you give everyone an opportunity to share their story and celebrate their differences, or declare a moratorium on the acknowledgment of all things, unlike mainstream actions?

Take this opportunity to establish some practices on how to acknowledge and celebrate your diversity. Review your culture and environment to ensure that tolerance and inclusion are woven into the fiber of the organization. Do a check of your policy manuals to make sure they include anti-discrimination clauses for LGBT employees. Make this an opportunity to remind all employees that your organization is a diversity-friendly organization (if indeed you are) that will not tolerate discrimination, exclusion, or insensitivity from one employee to another. Establish a safe environment for employees to have candid discussions about who they are without fear of reprisal or violating some antiquated notion of political correctness. Referring to a Black man, as "black" is not politically incorrect, it's a fact people. Last, but not least, allow employees to give feedback on how they feel the company is managing LGBT and equality within the workplace at large.

Don't be intimidated, promote participation

A break room or common area where employees are known to gather is the perfect spot to post your organization's commitment to equality, diversity, and inclusion statement, or information promoting opportunities to celebrate LGBT Pride Month. This makes employees aware of events but also emphasizes the company's stance on LGBT acceptance. Seek opportunities to partner with organizations that advocate for LGBT rights and people. There may be opportunities for your employees to volunteer, be a part of learning opportunities, and facilitate discussions and training to better understand issues related to human rights and the LGBT community at large. There is a disruption that needs to happen as we continue to strive for equality and inclusiveness that goes well beyond the rainbow. However, this is LGBT Pride Month, and it serves as a great opportunity for HR pros to lead the charge in reinforcing your organization's stance on tolerance and diversity in the workplace. HR leaders are in a unique position to take the discussion to the next level. Sure, it's so much easier to sit back and let the opportunity pass quietly; there is safety in homogeny. But does that really serve your organization and employees in the long run?

10. DIVERSITY: ARE WE THERE YET?

An auditor arrived for an ambush audit. He asked to speak with the individual who oversees HR – the receptionist called me. Minutes later, I entered the conference room where I had her seat him. I extended my hand and said, "Hi, I'm William Wiggins. I'm in charge of HR here; what can I do for you today?

He looked at my hand, looked me directly in the eye, and said: "I am waiting for the person in charge of HR. Will he be joining us?" Unfortunately, these moments are common for me. We awkwardly attributed the disconnect to the early morning hour coupled with him not yet having his coffee and trying to act like I had not been disrespected in my own office. Though common, moments like this continue to disrupt my comfort zone, in a good way, because I am reminded that there are miles to go before we reach the diverse promised land. Why did the auditor not make the connection between me and the individual in charge of HR? Why was I not worthy of a handshake even if I were impersonating an HR leader? Is it possible that a Black man in an HR leadership capacity is uncommon in this line of work, in a day and age where diversity is every organization's middle name? If so, why?

Diversity: what does that even mean?

Practically, the definition of diversity, per Merriam-Webster, is "the condition of having or being composed of differing elements; variety; especially the inclusion of different types of people (such as people of different races or cultures) in a group or organization." Theoretically, diversity predates the cavemen in practice; the evolution of diversity, not to mention the emphasis placed on it, is a much more recent (very recent) development.

Conceptually, diversity encompasses acceptance and respect. It does not simply mean tolerance; it means understanding that individuals are unique, and recognizing, respecting, and learning from those differences. These are differences along the dimensions of age, physical abilities, race, ethnicity, gender, religious beliefs, sexual orientation, socio-economic status, political beliefs, other ideologies, and even hobbies. It is fostering a climate where equality and mutual respect are intrinsic, not forced. It means leading your organization in establishing a set of intentional practices that involve:

- Fostering an environment of mutual curiosity and respect for qualities and experiences that are different from our own.

- Recognizing that personal, cultural, and institutionalized discrimination creates and sustains privileges for some while creating and perpetuating disadvantages for others.

- Building alliances despite differences so that we can work together to eliminate all forms of discrimination.

Diversity includes knowing how to relate to those qualities that are different from our own and outside the groups that we are both born and ascribed to. These groups can be age, ethnicity, class, gender, physical abilities, race, sexual orientation, as well as religious status, gender expression, educational background, geographical location, income, marital status, parental status, life and work experiences, etc.

Among the people that I have managed at one time or another, have been a self-identified vampire, a witch, a warlock, and Cleopatra reincarnated. I have also been blessed (and I mean that sincerely) to have employed a trapeze artist, a professional hugger, a burlesque performer, a reformed skinhead, and a Mama Cass impersonator for good measure. What I've learned from each of those individuals is that categories of difference are not always fixed but also can be fluid. Through my evolution as an HR leader, I've learned to respect an individual's right to self-identification and self-expression. I have even learned that differences can always be utilized productively.

I know that by now "diversity" may feel a bit like an overused buzzword; it certainly isn't a new concept. But let's be real; people haven't always been exactly warm and cozy toward those who differ from themselves in terms of backgrounds, life experiences, and identities… a brother couldn't even get a handshake from an external auditor in his own office, for whatever the reason. Discrimination based on race in the United States of America, the land of the free, and home of the brave wasn't officially deemed illegal until 1964. Since then, we have experienced 8 years of a Black president and are now governed by an orange one who self-identifies as a "nationalist." God Bless America! No judgment, just acknowledgment of the highs and lows of the diversity journey.

If 2019 is your year to set your organization on a path to diversity, begin with understanding the basics:

- **Gender Diversity**

  One's "sex" refers to one's biological makeup and the sex you were assigned at birth. Gender, on the other hand, is one's identification of self as male, female, a blend of both, and neither.

- **Sexual Diversity**

  Overwhelmingly, people consider gender and sexual orientation to be the same. Keep in mind that gender identity solely has to do with how we see ourselves. Sexual orientation, on the other hand, has more to do with how we relate to others.

- **Racial Diversity**

  Attitudes toward racial and ethnic diversity remain mixed. I hope you're sitting for this one–not all Americans embrace diversity believe immigrants play a valuable role in the development of our country or think that ethnic diversity makes the U.S. a better place to live. I know that sounds about as ridiculous as building a wall across the southern border of the United States (but not the northern) to keep out people with leprosy, terrorists, and coyotes.

- **Cultural Diversity**

  A much more personal type of diversity is cultural diversity. It has more to do with the norms, beliefs, and customs practices within a community and/or ethnic group. An employee could be of a certain race but may identify with an opposite culture.

One major way we as HR leaders can start chipping away at the significant work that remains undone in diversifying our workplaces is by creating a strategic diversity and inclusion implementation strategy, one that includes training, and creating policies that are thoughtful and impactful. Don't be afraid of offending or being paralyzed by political correctness. To do nothing is more offensive and detrimental to your organization.

Take opportunities to talk about your company's diversity goals and why it's important for the company to reach them. Talk about what your employees and organization will gain by being more diverse and how diversity will make your teams better. Reinforcing the importance of these goals to your leadership will get everyone moving in the same direction.

Regardless of your organization's focus and structure, fostering an environment of diversity and inclusiveness in your workplace will make your organization stronger and your people more invested in your mission.

Make the commitment. You stand to lose nothing but gain everything.

11. DEI: ARE WE GOING TO DO IT OR JUST TALK ABOUT IT?

Organizations should focus directly on who is represented in their workforce and who is included. We're done talking - it's time for action.

Are we all about creating Diversity, Equity, and Inclusion (DEI), or are we about the theatre of diversity, equity, and inclusion?

I've heard these words strung together so often by now, that not only has the spirit of DEI overshadowed the function of DEI, but we blend the words 'diversity, equity, and inclusion' so readily that they are becoming synonymous and thus in danger of being reduced to a task on a checklist. Without an understanding of these words as a part of our values, mission, and strategy, we are likely placing emphasis on the wrong efforts and suffering the consequences without even realizing it. By now we know that DEI is not likely to happen organically – it requires hard work and strategy. DEI is not a 'nice to have,' it's essential.

Organizations should focus directly on who is represented in their workforce and who is included. However, diversity efforts should not be confused with creating an inclusive environment. An inclusive environment has more to do with what it means to an individual present in an organization or environment. Organizations truly invested in diversity, equity, and inclusion should not only be probing to determine what it means for individuals of marginalized groups to be 'included' but also what 'included' means to their colleagues from dominant, advantaged, or privileged groups.

Second, organizations should be concerned with how underrepresented and marginalized employees view their participation in the organization and how their presence and contributions are received by others. When considering how equity features in your organization, know that issues of equity are often the underlying causes for why we need diversity initiatives in the first place. Equity considerations can be difficult to address because they often relate to deep-seated structural – often intentional – systems of inequality which are difficult to dispel, particularly wherever there are decision-makers within the organization that benefit from them. Equity initiatives should be focused more on changing the institutions of inequity, rather than supporting individuals inside the company to endure despite them. Therefore, organizations that are not prepared to take on equity considerations will see little progress toward diversity.

When DEI fails to launch

Simply making a declaration that your organization fosters diversity, equity, and inclusion or hiring someone to oversee your DEI initiatives will not be enough to make it a reality. Now more than ever, businesses are hiring Chief Diversity Officers.

While the increase in DEI-focused leadership sounds encouraging, many organizations have experienced a decrease in diversity hiring, as well as employee engagement around DEI.

Why? Because business leaders don't see DEI as a core business strategy, which leaves the DEI function within an organization often understaffed and under-resourced.

DEI leaders often find themselves un-empowered to make the kind of impact necessary to change the culture of the organization. One reason is that DEI remains in conflict with the organization's objectives and leaders are challenged to operate business-driven DEI metrics.

Desirable as DEI may (or may not) be to some, business leaders cannot see the return on investment. They are unable to make a clear connection between profitability and DEI. Another reason is the complexity of issues surrounding DEI. There are often underlying cultural issues within an organization that need to be properly addressed before diversity, equity, or inclusiveness can be achieved successfully.

Start your DEI initiative at the beginning

A good DEI initiative begins with good old-fashioned emotional intelligence, a baseline level of respect for marginalized populations, empathy, and an understanding of what they experience in an environment of individuals from dominant groups. It requires the capacity to envision a diverse and inclusive environment, which, truth be told, not all are ready for because to some it means compromising values and traditional practices that they hold near and dear. Therefore, the inability to truly advance a DEI initiative often leads to frustration and ultimately paralysis at all levels. Assess the current culture of your organization to determine what barriers might exist that may have traditionally contributed to the lack of diversity, equity, and/or inclusiveness. An organization steeped in unconscious bias cannot be expected to suddenly embrace DEI, not without first addressing that critical underlying issue.

The organization's executive leadership team needs to view DEI as a critical organizational objective that aligns with a value-driven business strategy that clearly identifies their expectations for how DEI will impact the business and strategy. An employee population with differences in race, age, gender, ethnicity, educational background, personality, and personal preferences can all be part of the strategic picture.

A diverse workforce and a culture fostering inclusivity may prove to be more innovative, collaborative, and creative, resulting in higher productivity. When the strategic value is identified and supported by the organization's senior leadership team from the top down, DEI becomes woven into the fiber of the organization. Anything less, and DEI remains an extra-curricular initiative.

In conclusion

Advancing DEI in a culture and environment where respect and acceptance are lacking, or your leadership team is not on board, will always yield poor outcomes. Know your organization and be realistic with your expectations.

CHAPTER 4

Performance

"First, we'll do a job performance preview."

1. EMPLOYEE DEVELOPMENT: A SOLID INVESTMENT

Why invest in employee development? The people of an organization collectively form its most vital resource and should be made to feel valued, relevant, and needed. Employees that are nurtured and developed can prove to be the foundation of an organization. Employee development also goes a long way toward building an attractive employer brand – showing an environment that many would strive to enjoy. Yet, if I've heard it once from managers, I've heard it a thousand times: "All I want is for people to come to work and do their job." Is that really all there is?

Good leaders develop exceptional people

People will come to work and do the job they are paid to do but if you intend to be a competitive, progressive organization, you must be committed to developing your employees into exceptional contributors and performers. This is the very core of your job as a leader. Employees of all backgrounds, generations, and professions want to feel that their managers genuinely care and are committed to developing and supporting their professional advancement and even their personal growth. Even if they do not express wanting (or are unclear of) a path to advancement, most employees want support, coaching, and the opportunity for betterment.

I was fortunate to have a great thought partner, manager, and mentor early in my career. I learned from her:

- the value of the diversity of people, ideas, and perspectives long before diversity was a buzzword.

- that true leaders concern themselves with the holistic experience of their employees.

- that putting people first does not mean putting the organization second, because they are one and the same.

- that a part of being a leader means also leading your people to success and being as proud of those successes as you are of your own

- if you are not willing to develop your people and bring them along on the journey, then you should get out of the way and let someone else do the job.

Employee development tips

Employee development is a long-term commitment and should not be confused with new employee orientation. When practiced consistently, it inspires loyalty, increased engagement, and a culture of high performers. When assessing how to get the most from your employees, start with some of the basics:

Offer professional training

The world is changing daily; make sure your employees are keeping up with the times. You want your team to be equipped with the latest and greatest innovations your industry has to offer; it only makes you stronger in the long run. Professional training doesn't necessarily have to be specific to the employee's current job or directly related to performing a task. It could be for a job that they may one day occupy. It could even be for training to develop one's ability to work strategically or hone their business acumen. If training is not a line item in the budget, start your program by requiring your employees to listen to one or two podcasts per week to keep up-to-speed with marketplace trends and new practices, strategies, and tactics that are tried and true. Start small by creating your own knowledge base of critical information and best practices to pass on to new hires as you grow your team. This will be time-consuming and even a bit tedious at first, but building a successful talent pool takes time.

Incorporate coaching and mentoring

While both are key components of developing your employee for the next level of their career, both are often neglected; thus, valuable knowledge, skills, and insights may not be passed on to the detriment of your organization. This should be a part of any leader's core job responsibilities. If they don't want to do it, they don't deserve the honor of being called a leader. As a leader, start engaging your employees. When coaching, remember to focus on concrete issues, (e.g., managing more effectively, speaking more articulately, learning how to think strategically, etc.). When mentoring, start by creating a safe environment where the employee is comfortable sharing whatever issues impact their personal and professional growth – an environment where they are not intimidated to provide feedback. Start the relationship by asking a few simple questions:

- What are your career objectives and how can I support you in meeting them?

- What would you like to learn that could help you maximize your performance?

- How can I support you in your personal development?

- What motivates you?

Mentor or coach? Here's why you need both

Be intentional about having regular dialogue to allow employees to reflect on their accomplishments and where you can support them in achieving their true potential. Start building your internal mobility and mentorship programs. This is where strong employer brands are made.

Never underestimate the value of EQ. For those that don't know, Emotional Intelligence (EQ) is our capacity as humans to recognize and validate the emotions of others as well as our own; and to use emotional information to guide thinking and behaviors. Emotional Intelligence is a gift and even though it drives everything that we do, the importance of EQ has been minimized in a great number of organizations. You have an opportunity to re-introduce this concept into the fiber of your organization. Self-awareness, empathy, and self-regulation should be desirable skills when identifying potential leaders. Get the ball rolling by asking questions like:

- How do you feel about your work?

- What are your current obstacles?

Your workforce needs to be seen, heard, acknowledged, validated, and cultivated, which are all needs that go unmet in too many work environments. The most supportive leaders are skilled at listening, and staying present to employee challenges can help elevate them both professionally and personally. Employee development is as critical as any technical skill, and it goes a long way toward building a cohesive successful team.

2. WHEN PERFORMANCE APPRAISALS GO BAD

What do you do when an employee, known to be a top performer, wants to file a grievance related to the performance appraisal process, someone who has achieved recognition as an innovator, received a collaboration award, and was on the fast track to a leadership role? It is a situation that would raise a red flag to any talent management leader. What could have happened during the performance appraisal process to spark such uncustomary upset?

Objective vs. subjective performance appraisals

In the scenario mentioned above, there were two contributing factors. First, the employee had been rated by a manager that they had worked for less than 60 days. Second, the feedback in the review centered around an isolated incident that occurred while the employee was on PTO only two weeks before the review. Sounds like a manager forgot the first rule of performance appraisals: one misdeed should not be the whole of one's performance appraisal.

No matter how well-defined the intention and objective of a performance appraisal are, more often than not they end up being subjective. As critical as the performance appraisal process is to an employee's growth and development, poor execution of this process (i.e., using it as a punitive measure or measuring performance without adequate data) serves no useful purpose and can cause more harm than good unless turnover is your objective, which is, unfortunately how this story ends.

Performance Appraisals 101

Performance appraisals should serve at least three useful proposes:

- To provide actionable feedback to each employee on their overall performance during a specific period of time.

- To highlight performance trends and determine the employee's potential for growth.

- To encourage or identify and resolve behaviors and performance trends to promote peak performance and development.

Primary problems with the performance appraisal system

Time and time again, employees go all year long with little to no feedback, that is, until their annual performance appraisal, which is often tethered to their compensation review. Suddenly, judgment is rendered for inadequacies long past vs. recognition for reliable performance. Is it unreasonable that an employee might receive feedback in the moment or at least quarterly to allow the employee to take corrective action on performance issues that might impact their growth or compensation?

Another common pitfall of performance appraisal is that they focus heavily on character traits that have been ascribed to the employee by their manager or reviewer, i.e., attitude, perceived level of ambition, positivity, personality, etc. While these factors may contribute to performance, oftentimes they become primary measures in assessing an employee's standing; and the notion that performance is about output quality, volume, dollar value, and responsiveness is all but forgotten. This can lead to a biased review, which can result in discrimination issues.

If it ain't one thing, it's the manager

Too many new managers do not receive performance appraisal training. We continue to take it for granted that this process is intuitive and that all managers are capable of giving feedback, which is actually an area where most managers are challenged. Feedback can be vague in order not to offend. Managers often artificially rate employees below what is required for a pay increase, to meet the budget, or to keep employees from being eligible for promotion (as part of that subjective judgment). Others will overrate low performance to avoid coaching or taking necessary disciplinary action. You know who they are.

Fixing the process: what's the first step?

Change the paradigm. Try moving not only toward evaluating the employee on what they have done but also on what they are capable of. Performance appraisals should be seen as a way of assessing an individual's strengths and weaknesses, and then assigning them tasks commensurate with their skills. Try developing a culture where managers are encouraged – if not required – to provide ongoing assessment of their employees. This will enable employees to make the required changes in real-time vs. learning about their shortcomings and failures 12 months later. Performance appraisals done poorly will most certainly adversely impact engagement, trust, collaboration, and turnover.

3. MEASURING PERFORMANCE REMOTELY. IMPOSSIBLE! OR IS IT?

Resist the urge to micromanage your remote (or any) employees' performance. The outcome will be turnover.

"How should I know how employees are performing? We're remote," said the people manager to the HR leader. HR teams have had to reinvent every aspect of the employee lifecycle. Performance management is no exception. If your organization was measuring performance prior to the pandemic, some key elements of effective performance management haven't changed. We've adapted to a new work world, created new policies and guidelines for doing business, and reduced our environmental footprint; some of us have even grappled with and conquered new maladies called Zoom fatigue, and social isolation.

Performance management in a remote environment may prove to be both easier and more rewarding than you think. Regular coaching conversations with one-on-ones and goal setting are the foundation of superior performance management in any organization, large or small. You'll be happy to know that all these elements can be conducted as effectively online, and using video conferencing tools as they can be face-to-face or in person.

Therefore, having the right digital and video conferencing platform to support the performance management process while giving you some level of face-to-face interaction to pick up on social cues and body language will be key.

Here are five things to consider when managing and performing in a remote or hybrid environment:

1. Communication builds trust

Communication is one of the most important aspects to consider while managing performance remotely. Remember that you're not physically with your remote staff as you would've been in an office environment. The absence of body language and gestures can make communication and assessment difficult. Building trust, particularly for remote performance assessments and appraisals, is essential. Allow and even encourage your employees to communicate freely without judgment. What happens on Zoom stays on Zoom! Use your one-on-ones and performance discussions as a forum for employees to bring to the table any barriers they are facing that might be impacting their performance and be prepared to help them adjust their work processes and strategies accordingly.

Fostering effective communication with your employees will cultivate better listening and more impactful feedback. Additionally, building trust will make your employee performance assessments less stressful and more engaging.

2. Be empathetic

Let's face it, remote working has its challenges. Keep in mind that the pandemic that launched this innovative approach to work and life has had a significant impact on our employees. Aside from no longer being at arm's length to resources and having immediate access to thought partners and impromptu team collaboration, your employees could be dealing with various struggles, such as taking care of their children and/or elderly. They may be adapting to remote work and a new work-life balance for the first time.

3. Embrace the new workspace; it's here to stay

Leaders need to release themselves from remote working biases toward employees you can't directly monitor or see in person every day. Such biases might impact your assessment of their performance. If you have someone that you are convinced is not working because you can't see them, either you need to shift your paradigm and practice a more progressive approach to managing performance, or you've hired the wrong person. Either way, it's on you. Resist the urge to micromanage your remote (or any) employees' performance. The outcome will be turnover. It's just that simple.

4. Focus on outcomes

Gone are the days when the early bird gets the worm. These were the days when employees were more concerned about being seen by the boss or playing the game of first in last out to be considered for promotion. If we had bothered to take a closer look when we all resided in one cubicle or another, we may have found that the hours an employee spends at their desk rarely correlate to performance. It can actually, on occasion, be an indicator of poor performance. With the rise in remote work, the concept of work-life balance became obsolete. In addition to encouraging boundaries to prevent burnout, keep your focus on outcomes rather than hours spent online. Establish annual or quarterly goals and objectives that are measurable and can be incorporated into your one-on-ones and performance appraisals. Drive a more productive discussion by keeping the conversation about output vs. perceived input.

5. Be present

Performance management is not a one-sided initiative. Although you're giving your employees feedback on their performance, listening can be as important as the feedback that you are giving. By listening to your employees, you can understand any challenges they might be experiencing in adapting to a more autonomous remote work lifestyle and deal with struggles they are facing that prevent them from performing at their best.

Sample questions to ask:

- What is one thing I can do to make your life better at work?

- Where would you like to be in six months?

- Describe a great day at work. What daily activities give you energy?

- What activities drain you?

- What big wins have you achieved since your last check-in?

- What is the most important thing you want to talk about today?

- What is your biggest challenge right now and how can I help?

- What obstacles are you facing and how do you plan to overcome them?

Asking these open-ended questions will allow the employee to detail any issues or barriers they are facing, but it also makes the employee feel valued during the assessment.

This helps make performance reviews a collaborative effort, boosts employee morale, and makes the discussion more collaborative.

So, if you want to know how your employees are performing in a remote environment-listen, learn, and provide the feedback that best supports them in their performance. Your feedback will be more actionable and will help them improve their performance.

4. PERFORMANCE MANAGEMENT 101: HOW DOES YOUR ORGANIZATION MEASURE UP?

An employee's annual salary review should not be the first time they are receiving feedback about their job performance. If an employee has been underperforming based on the expectation of the job, without feedback or coaching to improve from their manager, who is responsible for goals not being met? Whether or not performance is tied directly to salary increases and career advancement, employees should know how their performance is being measured. If you have a good performance management system that includes proper communication, there should be no surprises.

The purpose of a performance management system is to drive and promote performance within your organization. An effective process may be tied to your employee engagement initiative and should be focused on good constructive communication between managers and staff, with the sole purpose of developing strengths and maximizing the performance of the individual to achieve the organization's goals and objectives.

Some important steps and key components to building an effective performance management process include:

A. Creating and confirming the plan

Have a discussion to develop a plan around performance standards, and to detail the specific expectations of the employee based on the goals and objectives of the company.

B. Determining performance ratings

Develop a rating and scoring methodology that allows you to measure all employees consistently. Employees should understand the rating method and how their jobs will be measured prior to receiving feedback. Below is a more common performance management rating system scoring from 1 to 4:

1 = Does Not Meet Expectations

Performance is below standard expectations and requirements of the job. Overall performance improvement is required.

2 = Needs Improvement

Performance is inconsistent with the expectations and the requirements of the job. Further development may be required.

3 = Meets Expectations

Performance meets the expectations and the requirements of the job.

4 = Exceeds Expectations

Performance consistently exceeds the expectations and requirements of the job.

C. Being clear about performance goals

An effective performance management process should include a discussion where both the department and the organization's overall objectives are identified, correlated to individual objectives, and communicated to the employee. Having agreement on the desired goal, measurement, and period for completion at the beginning of the performance review process will lead to a more productive discussion with no surprises.

D. Providing constructive feedback

The feedback that managers provide to their employees should include observations and input from reliable sources about their performance in their ongoing jobs as well as any standout accomplishments.

E. Create opportunities for further development

A performance appraisal process that is not supported by a discussion for future learning and development for the employee will not be useful to the employee in meeting the individual or organization's goals and objectives.

The areas that are identified for development should be clearly defined, and the employee should be able to see how the new skills will be acquired and applied to the current and future job roles.

If the area of development is a requirement to achieve satisfactory performance in the current job role, then the plan for achieving the development must be clear to the employee.

Key components to a successful performance appraisal process

Involving the employees in the performance review process allows for greater engagement and ownership of the process and outcomes. Assessment and review of an employee's performance should not be punitive and should remain focused on facts, not emotion. Managers should be able to support the performance rating they assign. They must have a clear understanding of what would have made the performance scores higher or lower.

In making plans for future development, managers may include addressing specific requirements for current job performance or longer-term development for future roles. If an employee has been underperforming based on the expectation of the job, without feedback or coaching to improve, it is the manager who is responsible for goals not being met.

5. DON'T PUT INTERNAL MOBILITY ON THE BACK BURNER

I recently asked a colleague, "How is your internal mobility initiative going?" Her response - "We had to put all that on pause due to COVID-19 and all the staff who are tasked with D&I as a result of the protest." I was struck by how optional such a key talent initiative becomes during times of disruption (real or perceived). Internal mobility is about having the right talent on hand to meet organizational goals and being prepared to respond to the unexpected as it happens.

The very definition of internal mobility is that it enables organizations to rapidly adapt to changing environments, with the ability to deploy and move key skills across projects, businesses, and borders when needed. What better time than now to have an agile employee pool to support your organization's needs? Having a defined internal mobility initiative, shouldn't tax your organization's resources or compete with other organizational objectives. It should bolster better outcomes through more streamlined processes and increased productivity. Without a doubt, your current employee population is infused with high-quality candidates that are consistently overlooked by your TA team. Creating an internal pool of qualified, upwardly mobile employees enables you to fill vacant positions faster at a fraction of the cost of recruiting or sourcing externally and helps create a solid employer brand through resulting employee engagement.

Jumpstart your internal mobility initiatives

If the current state of affairs has you redefining the footprint of your workspace or spotlighting your diversity and inclusion commitments, consider jump-starting your internal mobility initiatives by simply incorporating the following five techniques to engage and build your internal candidate pipeline.

Make it an organizational objective to combine the TA function with HR.

In order to understand and identify opportunities for internal mobility, TA has to be a part of the discussion around employer branding, staff engagement, succession planning, and career pathing – not just recruiting. Effective career pathing is one of the most underutilized opportunities to tap into the full potential of your existing workforce while also helping to increase engagement and retention. Encourage recruiters to take part in career development discussions and to foster strong relationships with your business leaders to develop a thorough understanding of their talent needs, both current and future state, and to leverage TA or other technologies to facilitate greater information sharing across HR functions (e.g., talent, performance, learning, and career).

Create and nurture an environment of internal mobility.

Promoting internal mobility should be a part of a larger more systemic approach to talent sourcing. It begins with developing effective ways to promote professional growth and embedding it into organizational culture. Organizations should include the TA function in critical conversations about current employees and their career experiences. Taking these steps can allow an organization to invest confidently in its own people. High-performing talent acquisition teams recognize the value of internal mobility. The most effective internal talent pools support transparent talent mobility – a dynamic process for moving talent from role to role – at the leadership, professional, and operational levels.

Identify an executive sponsor to champion your internal mobility efforts.

Provide clarity around the value of mobility and promote it to support employee growth and create engaging worker experiences. If you don't already have one, create a more formalized process for employees to discuss their career goals with their peers and leaders and make sure they are engaged in frequent and transparent conversations about the preferred skills and experiences necessary for success while identifying a pathway to those necessary tools and pieces of training.

Cultivate an internal talent pool

Internal talent pools are a critical component of an organization's talent pipeline. High-performing organizations proactively nurture relationships with internal talent to understand their long-term career objectives. Business leaders and recruiters leverage these insights and collaborate to cultivate talent from within and further reinforce that the culture supports and encourages internal mobility.

Join forces with your business leaders.

See to it that your TA team and business leaders are effectively working together regarding the people, positions, and profiles of success on their respective teams. Encourage recruiters to routinely engage with internal applicants as a part of their standard work. This creates an opportunity for TA teams to better understand the goals and motivations of the internal applicant.

Internal mobility provides avenues for all staff to progress and evolve within an organization, not just those identified as "high potential." A solid program can support an organization in developing and aligning its workforce to strategic business needs. I would argue it is a critical component of success in hard times and should always be a key focus of talent teams.

6. HOW IMPORTANT ARE INTERNAL MOBILITY AND CAREER PATHING

I could see the buzz from my window on the 33rd floor. There were multiple ambulances, local news, and the works. Moments later I received a call that one of our employees had attempted suicide. After receiving a phone call that left the employee inconsolable, she rose from her desk, took the elevator downstairs, walked across the street, and jumped off a nearby bridge into the river beneath. Thankfully, she survived. The reason she provided to her rescuers was – "I didn't get the promotion, again."

This employee certainly had other issues beyond a stagnating career, but it got me thinking… Could a career pathing failure be the last straw for an employee who is on the edge?

What is career pathing?

Career pathing is the process of creating an action plan for an employee to follow that best supports career development within, and sometimes beyond, the organization of their employment. This process is most successful when it involves Human Resources, the employee's direct supervisor, other potential managers within the organization, and, of course, the employee. Career pathing focuses on identifying vertical and lateral opportunities for advancement or progression for an employee, as well as the skills and competencies necessary for success in each new role. When done properly, career pathing significantly improves employee engagement, contributing to a culture of engagement and a stable work environment.

Promoting this process among employees will benefit the organization by identifying skill gap shortages. It also provides detailed insight into various paths for advancement and ensures that opportunities for growth, learning, and personal fulfillment are accessible to each employee in an organization, from entry-level to upper management. With over 40% of the workforce looking for higher compensation, career advancement opportunities, or even work-life balance, having a defined career pathing program – and a visible commitment to your employees to promote from within – keeps your high-potential employees committed to the organization. Does internal mobility build a progressive organization?

External hires are certainly made more frequently, however, there are multiple benefits to promoting from within an organization. External candidates can indeed bring fresh ideas to the organization yet internal candidates are already steeped in the mission, product knowledge, and culture and are familiar with or have performed some duties of the position that they seek. There is evidence that promoting from within is not only less costly than external hiring but internally promoted employees are also better performing, more motivated, and more engaged.

Ready to launch your own career pathing initiative or improve your internal mobility processes? Here are three things to help you build your case.

Improve employee productivity

Evidence shows that disengaged employees cost employers 4 to 6 billion dollars in lost productivity each year.

According to Gallup, implementation of an internal promotion or career pathing initiative has positively impacted employee engagement well beyond the average of 33% (in some instances, as high as 70%). When employee engagement rises, profitability and productivity will inevitability follow. The more engaged employees are, the fewer leave days are taken, fewer missed days, and lower turnover costs. In other words, career pathing can have a profound impact on your employee productivity and your bottom line.

Increase employee retention

One of the most common reasons employees leave a job is a lack of career growth opportunities. Gone are the days when employees were content with working an eight-hour shift, receiving a paycheck, major medical, retirement fund, and a gold-plated watch at the end of it all. Today's workforce is made up of evolved baby boomers, millennials, and overachieving types who would just as soon build a spreadsheet on a mobile phone from a coffee shop than sit behind a desk for an hour. They want personal and professional fulfillment – to learn and grow in a position that enables them to utilize their strengths. According to Gallup's most recent State of the American Workplace Report, "Growth and Development are still at the top of an employee's wish list." If employees feel there are barriers to their progression within their current organization, they are likely to leave.

Enhance Succession Planning and Longevity

Consider tasking your leaders with identifying and coaching high-potential employees across a variety of roles and departments to take over key positions as a part of their standard work. Invest! Evaluate your employees to identify those with the greatest potential to advance within the organization. Once you have identified those with high potential, you can then offer them the appropriate training and development necessary to set them up for success. This enables the organization to move high-potential employees into key positions efficiently with as little downtime as possible.

Empowered and engaged employees are essential to the long-term success of an organization. Building an effective career pathing program, if done properly, will prove to be one of your greatest investments in resources.

CHAPTER 5

Recruiting

"O.K., I'm good for I.T.—how about spreadsheets, anybody here good at spreadsheets?"

1. "DO YOU LIKE ESSENTIAL OILS?" IS NOT A LEGITIMATE INTERVIEW QUESTION

After being twenty minutes late for our long-awaited connection, she opened the conversation with:

- "About me, prior to coming here, I worked at a day spa."

- "Do you like essential oils?"

- "I feel like we've met before?"

- "Oh, November is your birthday? That's Sagittarius; I'm a stereotypical Capricorn."

- "Do you have any pets or young children? Good, because we work super long hours."

- "I'm a biking geek; do you bike? This team is super picky when it comes to biking and fitness."

- "You graduated college in 1984? You don't sound that old!"

- "What are you reading? I'm reading "Fifty Shades of Gray"; I know I'm such a dork!"

You're probably wondering why I'm detailing my experience at the local speed-dating chapter. I'm not. The commentary and questions were part of an infamous phone interview I had for a management position. What began as a prime opportunity to work for one of the world's leading online retailers, became the rock bottom of candidate experiences for me.

The backstory – this occurred after three separate no-shows and missed connections all on the part of the hiring manager, who on one occasion confessed that she knew she had a phone interview but opted to go biking instead. "I thought someone would have let you know; my bad!" was the apology – and the encounter ended, thank goodness, with "Awesome! We'll be in touch."

Nearly two months later, I received a call from the recruiter to schedule a face-to-face meeting for the same job now that the hiring manager was "back from her trip to Thailand"; in a moment of complete clarity, I realized that this process had more twists and turns than the Amazon... and I wanted off this ride. So, then and there, I removed myself from the process.

The problem

Despite the existence of EEO laws, created largely to promote fairness and to mitigate discrimination of any kind in hiring practices, we still have untrained hiring managers and recruiters asking questions that are illegal and irrelevant to job performance. Interview questions should be designed to determine a candidate's capability to perform the essential functions of the job as defined in the job description, not to find out if the candidate prefers boxers or briefs.

The fix

The first step in fostering a fair, ethical, and legal interview process is having an HR department that keeps their hiring managers and recruiters trained and current on the latest legal hiring practices. Standardize your interview process for consistency and consider offering training on best interviewing practices for your hiring managers/staff charged with interviewing your candidates. Let's start with teaching the basics.

Questions that are illegal and non-job related:

- What religion are you?

- Are you married?

- I see you were in the military. What type of discharge did you receive?

- Is Spanish your first or second language?

- How old are you?

- What year did you graduate high school/college?

- How did you injure yourself?

- Do you have any medical problems that would interfere with your work here?

- Do you rent or own your home?

- How is your commute from all the way down there?

Standard interview questions that can be asked of all applicants:

- If hired, can you provide proof that you are legally authorized to work in the US?

- Are you able to fulfill the requirements of this job with reasonable accommodation?

- Are you at least 18 years old (if that is your company's policy or an applicant needs to be a certain age for legal reasons)?

- Can you work Sundays, Christmas, and Easter (if those are viable shifts)?

Casual questions to steer clear of and that could later be troublesome:

- Do you bike or work out?

- What are you reading?

- Do you have any hobbies?

- Do you like essential oils?

The benefit of implementing a standardized process

Developing and maintaining a standardized process and questions for interviewing to evaluate candidates will not only improve the candidate experience, but it will also lower your organization's risk of scrutiny and legal landmines. The ultimate advantage of a standardized, fair, and compliant process is that it helps the interviewer gather focused, relevant data to match the right person to the right job, yielding better hiring results, without question.

2. WHY DOES EVERYONE THINK THEY CAN RECRUIT BETTER?

Can someone tell me **WHY IN THE WORLD EVERYONE THINKS THEY CAN RECRUIT BETTER THAN THE RECRUITER?** I looked up to see my clearly disturbed star recruiter standing in the doorway of my office. I asked him what the matter was. An emotional recount of a situation revealed that he had, for the fourth time in as many weeks, been yelled at and had his very competence publicly questioned by two hiring managers from the same team.

In one instance, he had been admonished for suggesting that forwarding all 100-plus applicants for a position was not an efficient way to partner. In another instance, he had been sternly admonished by the other hiring manager for not forwarding an applicant who did not meet the minimum qualifications for the role. The role called for specific medical coding certification and terminology. The applicant had no certifications, no formal education beyond high school, and 3 months as a census taker. On this day, during another exchange, the recruiter was yelled at for pushing back on one of the hiring managers insisting that a job be posted just long enough for an internal applicant, who just happened to be on FMLA, to apply before taking it down. This encounter ended with the hiring manager yelling at the recruiter, "I'm sick of having to do your job for you."

I couldn't take it anymore. I called the most recently offending hiring manager, and it was on! At the crescendo of the verbal scuffle, I said to the hiring manager, "It is no more acceptable for you to mandate how my recruiter performs his job than it would be for him to tell you to change your therapeutic approach to a patient." Not only did the hiring manager look at me as if he had never thought of it that way before, but he also said it out loud. Right before I could have sworn I heard a celestial choir sing out. And so began a more reasonable discussion about the role of a recruiter. Determining the relationship between recruiter and hiring manager

The recruiter's role has long since shifted from being an order taker for the hiring manager, to presenting information as an advisor and consultant. They are not there to serve the hiring manager but to collaborate and partner with the hiring manager. Both are working toward the same goal It's OK for the recruiter to advise "You don't need these 100 things in a candidate; you only need these five things."

Communication is key. Some hiring managers will insist on circumventing the system or talking about a position every day—even when a less frequent cadence is necessary. It's for the recruiter to understand and drive how much and what type of communication is needed. Try committing to windows of time for reviewing resumes, conducting interviews, and following up with the hiring managers. Neither the recruiters nor the hiring manager should ever leave each other guessing or wondering what the other is up to. Don't leave room for the imagination to create the story. Own your profession, unapologetically, especially if you are a recruiter. Recruiting is not a job, it's a profession that requires skill, strategic agility, and a level of technical expertise which – contrary to popular belief – is not intrinsic for everyone.

[It's not just about the candidate; how's your hiring manager experience?]

In conclusion. A mutual respect for one's professional expertise is at the root of any good organizational partnership. No one should be made to feel subjugated in any given partnership by way of their profession, particularly the partner in the end-to-end process of acquiring top talent for your organization.

3. IF IT'S NOT ONE THING, IT'S THE RECRUITER

However, it can be a significant problem for recruiters and the hiring managers they partner with to drive talent. Find out what it takes and commit yourself to integrating employee experience into your recruiting strategy. I received a call from an irate hiring manager demanding the termination or, at the very least, a performance improvement plan for one of my most seasoned and talented recruiters. A requisition for a hard-to-fill role had been open for 22 days with no qualified applicants. That is except for two that we lost to competitors when the hiring manager himself was not able to interview either candidate due to a bike race that took him out of state for five of 22 days.

I was even warned if I did not 'take action,' the matter would be escalated to the top, which as far I knew, was me. Having heard enough. I retorted, 'Why stop at a performance improvement plan? Why not shackle him to a pillory in the lobby and pelt him with rotten produce for all to see?' The conversation in a flash shifted to my sarcasm, which thankfully the hiring manager hated more than he did the recruiter. It did, however, provide a momentary deflection, just long enough for me to shift to a more realistic discussion, one that did not vilify the recruiter as the reason for not being able to find labor on demand.

To hiring managers and organizations, everywhere – I implore you to breathe! Stop blaming your recruiter for the state of this unprecedented labor market. They are not the enemy.

We are experiencing a tight job market during a time when job openings outnumber job seekers. So far, we have survived one of the worst pandemics on record and, somehow, emerged with a record number of job openings. Per the Bureau of Labor Statistics, we will have more than 20 million job openings in the US in 2022, bringing the percentage of unfilled jobs to one in eight. The good news is the pool is saturated with qualified talent. The bad news is demand for labor is also historically high. A booming job market is music to the ears of applicants. However, it can be a significant problem for recruiters and the hiring managers they partner with to drive talent. The disruption of virtual workplaces became the norm during a time when workplace culture, mission, and core values became paramount to job seekers, along with flexibility and balance – all of which are new factors in the negotiation process for recruiters to contend with. People are no longer looking for a job – they are looking for an experience. Layer on the Great Resignation, and the pay compression that resulted; and it's clear that the labor shortage has emerged from a culmination of events, not your talent acquisition partners. While it is easy to blame the recruiter for empty seats, it is simply not their fault.

Things may get worse before they get better

What we know is that the past two years have changed the job market forever. While the future remains unpredictable, much of how we mitigate the impact of labor challenges is well within our control:

Focus on retaining the employees you have

Prioritize building retention strategies that include redefining the employee experience and understanding the impact of fostering an environment of well-being and belonging. Leaders should focus more on retaining their good employees. This requires examining their corporate culture, compensation packages, technology, and company policies from the perspective of retaining, rather than just attracting, employees.

Change your paradigm

Even as many organizations struggle to find talent, they remain unwilling to recognize that the workplace looks, feels, and operates very differently than it did two years ago, and they choose to hold on to their 'old ways' of doing business, which oddly enough has little to do with creating a positive employee experience that is not strictly about profitability, but is also about treating people well and creating a culture that sells itself. It is about becoming the organization that job seekers are drawn to and actively seek out. Find out what it takes and commit yourself to integrating employee experience into your recruiting strategy.

Focus on culture and leadership

Start engaging your recruiting and talent acquisition teams as strategic partners; they deserve no less. Recruiters align the right people to the right roles. Your recruiter can be your best asset when combatting a tough labor market. Not only do they have a broader perspective of your organization's culture and can more readily persuade a candidate what differentiates you from your competitors but they also have a deep understanding of the labor, and the ability to proactively source candidates using any number of the tricks of their trade.

They are often well connected, have multiple ways to achieve an organization's labor objectives, and are eager to work with their hiring managers at a higher level beyond the administrative.

Conclusion

Build relationships with your talent acquisition team and examine your objectives around the employee experience priority. No business can survive without labor. Convincing candidates to join your organization grows more challenging daily. Make supporting the team with the expertise to overcome those challenges a part of your long-term HR strategy.

4. TALENT ACQUISITION 101: IS THIS POSITION REMOTE?

What's the compensation range for this position? Is parking included? How about relocation? Just two years ago these were commonly asked questions of talent acquisition teams. The use of 'basic Zoom' rarely featured in the recruiting process, and many job offers were declined due to exorbitant commute times and expenses. So, what changed? A global pandemic hit, and the world was at home during prime time and witnessed the killing of George Floyd on television.

For the first time in history, job seekers wanted to know about an organization's commitment to safety in the workplace, social justice, and diversity. I'm talking about diversity beyond the occasional ethnic dish buffet that usually surfaced in breakrooms coast to coast, typically around the holidays. If your organization changed its strategy around acquiring and retaining talent with minimal disruption, seemingly overnight – kudos to you, but that may have been the easy part. Understanding and responding to the need for constant innovation in this strange new world of remote work and virtual connectivity is a bit more complex.

The talent pool just got a lot bigger, and a lot less dependent on location, with many organizations currently working in a remote or hybrid model. Does this mean that hiring will be easier? Not necessarily. A broader talent pool also means that more organizations are competing for candidates everywhere with geography no longer considered as a qualifier. This competition means organizations need to be strategic about their virtual processes and practices, from interviewing and onboarding, through the employee engagement process. How has the pandemic impacted talent acquisition and talent management?

By now we have all heard of the 'Great Resignation,' a movement that has led employees across all industries to look at their careers and what is important to them based on contemporary societal issues. The bad news is that this overdue change came bundled with a pandemic. Sheltering-in-place orders gave many workers the headspace to pause and consider, among other things, an environment more conducive to their health and well-being.

This movement also resulted in some significant life changes for some, including leaving their jobs, retirement, and extended sabbaticals to pursue lifelong passions, and for some, changing industries altogether, thereby further squeezing an already tight talent market.

Organizations were not only forced to implement more rigorous sourcing and recruiting processes to keep candidate pipelines active but to also consider alternative and innovative ways to engage and retain top talent, which is critical for organizations that want to stabilize their workforce in a complex job market that will only grow more competitive in the coming months.

What have we learned from the past two years?

We learned that the only thing we can predict is the unpredictable. Zoom fatigue and expanding waistlines aside, what we know for certain is that the preference for comfort and remote and hybrid workspaces is widespread and rapidly increasing. We know that the 'Great Resignation' (a by-product of COVID-19) has provided exposure to a more diverse and adaptable candidate pool, one that has been traditionally motivated by compensation, and stock options. With some surveys showing more than 70% of employees wanting flexible remote work options to continue past the pandemic, we know that workers are now driven and motivated by a wider range of factors, which include the culture of an organization, their commitment to diversity and social justice, and to what extent they can mitigate an employee's commute by offering alternative work models.

We can count on tech companies to continue to launch expanded platform offerings to support HR teams in optimizing the performance of their talent management systems from applicant tracking, and performance management, to measuring employee engagement.

Investing in technology, like video interviewing software and online onboarding platforms, can help ease the path in the virtual hiring process. Many organizations have implemented digital interviews and other platforms during the pandemic. With some organizations transitioning to indefinite remote or hybrid work models as a matter of safety or convenience, these methods are here to stay.

As our recruitment teams fine-tune their virtual interview processes and implement other digital-forward recruiting practices, we should also keep the candidate experience in mind and make sure that application processes are streamlined and intuitive, with great user interfaces, particularly since more people are applying for jobs on mobile devices.

Keeping DEI relevant

Now more than ever organizations are struggling with how to reconcile the dynamics of remote work with the environment required for effective DEI work. While DEI can be a bit more complex, remember that even though today's environment is more distributed and virtual, there must be a solid commitment and willingness on behalf of the organization to dedicate time for ongoing learning, and a cultural commitment to improvement. Make use of online platforms like Traliant to support your remote DEI training, and despite remote DEI being a challenge, make sure that embracing the challenges around both building internal DEI capacity and ensuring diverse, equitable, and inclusive practices across your organization are among your core objectives.

The impact of remote or hybrid models on work culture

Keep in mind that every interaction between the candidate and HR can impact your brand for years to come. These days, your opportunity to communicate your values, who you are as an organization, and the culture that you foster is done primarily via email, phone, and video.

Organizations will rise or fall based on how well they manage this complex juncture in the employee experience. Consider collaborating with marketing to strategize over developing digital marketing collateral, creating new content for social media, or updating your public online content to better communicate your values, culture, and the experience of working at your company.

This is a great time to be in HR! You have an opportunity to be more intentional, strategic, and creative about building your employees by having to accentuate the characteristics that make your culture unique, using alternative media vs. in-person interactions.

How you support your HR and Talent teams in messaging your strengths will help attract candidates who will appreciate what your organization has to offer and will thrive once they're on board. Ultimately, the new remote and hybrid environment could be an important advantage in attracting and retaining exceptional employees.

5. RECRUITING, COMPENSATION, BENEFITS, AND HUMAN RESOURCES – A CRITICAL PARTNERSHIP

As much as we all favor our respective Human Resource Management disciplines, it's time to give credit where credit is due. They are ALL critical to the success of an organization, particularly in today's staffing environment where companies are clamoring to attract and retain the best and the brightest talent to meet their business objectives. No matter how technically efficient a company becomes there is no greater asset to a company than its human capital when it comes to managing efficiency.

As we all know, humans like to be motivated, appreciated, and paid. Building loyalty, trust, and engagement among employees is not an endeavor to be compartmentalized. It takes a comprehensive HR team partnership representing Recruiting, Benefits & Compensation, and Human Resources to do it successfully. The absence of one of these HR partners makes the team less effective, and the employee experience becomes marginalized.

Recruiting, where the employee experience begins

In 2015, filing a job cost an average of $4,000 and took an average of 52 days,[1] making it necessary for employers to explore ways to proactively optimize recruiting practices and focus on retention so that changing jobs is not the fastest way to a promotion, more compensation, better benefits, or better working conditions. The recruitment process is an employee's first opportunity to form an opinion of a company. Candidates who have a negative experience during the recruiting phase of their experience will never forget it. It can cloud their perception of all other experiences going forward. Recruiting functions to ensure that the right people are being staffed in the right positions based on their abilities and the expressed needs of the company and hiring manager. The efficiency and viability of any company start with attracting the right talent. Therefore, the recruiting process plays a crucial role in the success of a company. How well they are able to source, screen, assess, and move prospective talent through a complicated process can have a significant impact on a company's ability to do business efficiently and profitably.

The impact of benefits and compensation

Compensation is the employer's way of expressing how they feel about the worth and value of the employee and the position. It typically refers to salary, or the financial compensation agreed upon between the employee and employer for the job. Benefits are in most cases considered a non-financial form of compensation offered in addition to salary. Employees today are motivated and incentivized as much by benefits as they are by salary. Trends show they are often more interested in the total value of their compensation and benefits and extra perks vs. salary. A company's ability to meet the demand for comprehensive compensation or an attractive Total Rewards package that includes extra perks or 'fringe benefits' is key to remaining competitive and attractive to today's talent pool. A solid employee-centric collaborative partnership between recruiting and compensation and benefits is key to identifying how best to appeal to candidates.

Human resources: maintaining engagement We've hired the right talent in the right role, with an agreeable compensation package, but there's still work to be done. There are many reasons why an employee may be motivated to call a company home – the opportunity for greater upward mobility, opportunities for learning and development, or greater compensation and benefits – are just a few examples. A strategic Human Resources team is one that is perpetually assessing their employee community, reviewing turnover metrics, and conducting a review of the market to identify innovative ways to engage and retain their talent which directly correlate to decreased turnover cost, lower absenteeism, and an increase in overall revenue. Companies with employee engagement programs achieve a 26% greater year-over-year increase in annual company revenue, compared to those who do not have formal programs.

An HR team that works collaboratively to anticipate and understand the needs of employees before the recruiting process begins is more likely to attract engaged committed talent to the workplace, which is essential to business success.

CHAPTER 6

Compliance

*"Do you think now that we're doing fewer illegal things
we can scale back the legal department?"*

1. HAS TITLE VII OF THE CIVIL RIGHTS ACT OF 1964 OUTLIVED ITS USEFULNESS? REALLY?

I was delivering EEOC training when the next slide was Protected Classes. I noticed some quizzical looks and furrowed brows in the audience, so I gave a broad definition of Protected Class and went on to define Title VII of the Civil Rights Act; the most important federal statute banning discrimination in the workplace. I went on to explain that Title VII creates protected classes of individuals, including classes based on age, religion, gender national origin, and race, and additionally, Title VII also forbids discrimination based on "color."

Someone raised their hand and informed me that race and color were the same. Using myself as an example, I informed the individual that race and color are in fact different.

My race is Black, and my color is dark brown, actually more like a dark mocha I'd say. While discrimination claims based on color are fewer, people have been denied employment opportunities based on – wait for it – the actual color of their skin. Not so shocking if you are a dark brown or mocha-colored man or woman who works for a living. I cited a claim filed by a server who was told that she was "too Black" (literally) for a management position. Her manager hypothesized that dark-skinned employees were not as dependable – I am assuming no tangible metrics were provided.

While the manager employed many Black people, there was overwhelming evidence to support that darker-skinned employees experienced a marked lack of progression and were not promoted into management or senior roles. The manager made employment decisions based on skin color, not race. Under Title VII, discrimination based on color is prohibited. The sad truth: this was a recent claim.

The audience went on to ask me to define the difference between Sex and Gender, and Sexual Orientation and Gender Expression. The discussion brought to the surface the need to redefine the protected classes succinctly as follows:

- **Race** – Federal civil rights laws do not define race. However, individuals may self-identify within certain ethnic and racial categories, including multiracial. All racial categories are protected under Title VII.

- **Color** – refers to the pigmentation of one's skin. An individual can make an allegation of color discrimination or color harassment against someone of the same race or color.

- **National Origins** – refers to a person's (or a person's ancestors') place of origin or the physical, cultural, or linguistic characteristics of an ethnic group.

- **Sex and Gender** – sex refers to the anatomy and biology that determines whether one is male, female, and/or intersex. Gender refers to the social constructs surrounding gender roles.

- **Gender Expression** – refers to how a person represents or expresses one's gender to others through external appearance, characteristics, or behaviors typically associated with a specific gender.

- **Sexual Orientation** – refers to the physical or emotional attraction toward a certain sex or gender. Additionally, individuals are protected from discrimination or harassment based on a perception of an individual's sexual orientation, even if that perception is mistaken.

- **Disability** – refers to a physical or mental impairment that substantially limits one or more major life activities of an individual. The policy also protects individuals who are regarded as having a disability or who have a record of a disability.

- **Pregnancy** – refers to individuals who are pregnant, just gave birth to a child, or suffer a medical condition as a result of pregnancy or childbirth are all protected.

- **Veteran Status** -Refers to anyone who serves or who has served in any branch of the United States armed forces, including students in the Reserve Officer Training Corps (ROTC). Volunteers for military duty must be treated the same as those who are ordered to active duty.

- **Age** – refers to discriminating against individuals because of their age. Students are protected from age discrimination in academic situations like admissions decisions and residence hall assignments, regardless of their age. An employee must be 40 years or older to fall within the protected category.

- **Religion/Creed** – refers to religious, moral, or ethical beliefs that are sincerely held and include all aspects of religious observance and practice.

- **Political Philosophy** – refers to a person's belief or endorsement of any system of thought pertaining to public policy or the administration of governmental functions.

- **Political Affiliation** – refers to a person's membership or association with others in a commonality of political purpose and support.

These definitions helped my audience get over the initial shock that life is not intrinsically fair, and behind each protected class are real cases of individuals who were denied some essential opportunity because of who they were, where they were born, what they believed in, and yes, even the color of their skin.

Finally, the question was asked, "I wonder if Title VII has outlived its usefulness as society has become more progressive?" The word on the street is in 2017 the Department of Justice, under the Trump administration, reversed the Obama-era policy that used Title VII to protect transgender employees from discrimination. Outlived its usefulness, perhaps to some?

As the push to "Make America Great Again" continues, I encourage you to brush up on your Title VII and be sure to train your managers accordingly. Make sure they are versed in this legislation and are trained to spot the potential risk and EEO violations, unintended or otherwise.

2. LISTENING FOR SEXUAL HARASSMENT

"Oh, my goodness! He's so nasty; what a pervert, I was so creeped out…" was just some of the water cooler commentary I would hear about one supervisor I worked with many years ago. I was mildly curious about what he had done or said to garner such consternation from our female employees, but mostly I ignored the comments. I thought poor soul, he had somehow made his way to the bad side of my omnipotent, omniscient administrative assistant in particular and there was no coming back.

I noticed a change in her routine, so I commented on how early she had been arriving at work. She responded, "I've been coming in extra early, so I don't have to wonder where he is lurking. When I saw him hiding behind the tree that morning, it shook me up." That got my attention. I asked, "Who in the world is hiding behind a tree, and why didn't you say something?" She responded, "I've been trying to tell you." For the first time, I thought "Could this be harassment?" I invited her into my office. That is where she placed Pandora's box on the conference table and opened it.

For months she had been subjected to blatant and unspeakable harassment at the hands of her colleague, a man she crossed paths with multiple times a day. Desperate to escape his advances, physical, and "nasty talk," she'd actually altered her schedule to avoid being stalked like prey in the parking lot as she was arriving and leaving work. I heard her making statements about him to the effect that he was "creepy," and "perverted" but took the characterizations as her personal assessment, without inquiring how she had come to them. I was a new manager at that point in my career and her direct supervisor.

Ultimately, an investigation was done, and the employee was dismissed, but I often reflect on that incident, and I ask myself, "Why did I not respond sooner? Why did it take my employee changing her work hours to get my attention? Why did I not hear her sooner?

I had heard it all myself in the workplace. I have often not been afforded the same level of respect or conventional considerations as my counterparts. I've been asked about the most intimate details of Black sexuality and subjected to behavior so foul that words wouldn't do it justice. As a matter of survival, I have developed a toughness and a tolerance for indiscretion and inappropriateness.

However, no matter how shameful or ridiculous the comments or behaviors are, I have never felt fearful for my safety, or livelihood, nor have I been not in control of the situation. Was it fair for me to expect my employees or others to adopt my tolerance based on my experiences? The bigger question was whether I allowed my personal experience to impact my responsiveness to my employees.

As my career evolved from Benefits to Human Resources and Staff Relations, knowing what I know now, I have often reflected on that unfortunate ordeal as a lesson learned. My years in Human Resources have refined my listening skills and sharpened my perspective when it comes to the employees I serve. Is it ever acceptable to get used to sexual harassment or inappropriateness in the workplace?

Let's re-educate ourselves

Title VII of the Civil Rights Law of 1964 prohibits, discrimination on the basis of sex, and sexual harassment, regarded as a form of sexual discrimination, can be defined as follows:

Unwelcome sexual advances, requests for sexual favors, and other verbal or physical harassment of a sexual nature. Harassment does not have to be of a sexual nature, however, and can include offensive remarks about a person's sex. Both the victim and the harasser can be either a woman or a man, and the victim can be the same sex.

Harassment is illegal when it is so frequent or severe that it creates a hostile or offensive work environment or when it results in an adverse employment decision (such as the victim being fired or demoted).

Employer liability

Employers are strictly liable for harassment of an employee by an owner or high-level manager. This means if one owner or manager harasses an employee, even without the knowledge of the other owners or managers, the employer is nevertheless legally responsible.

Employers may be strictly liable for harassment by a lower-level manager, or by a supervisor, if that supervisor has a sufficient degree of control over the working conditions of the victim. This means that the employer may be legally responsible for such harassment, even if no owner or manager knew about it.

Employers may be liable for the harassment of an employee's co-worker if the employer knew or should have known about the harassment and failed to take action. This means the employer will be liable if the employer was negligent in preventing or stopping the harassment.

If an employee complains of harassment to any supervisor or manager, the knowledge of the supervisor or manager will be considered to be the knowledge of the employer.

Check your policies

Sexual Harassment may result in a lengthy, costly, legal action and can also trigger an enforcement action by the EEOC. As HR leaders, we are bound to protect our employees first and foremost by having comprehensive policies and procedures defining sexual harassment, clearly defining a safe respectable process for an employee to lodge a complaint, and timely and thorough investigation of an employee's complaint. We are also obligated to educate employees and managers alike about sexual harassment policies and procedures, not only for the protection of the employee but also as a function of compliance.

Conclusion

Don't wait for employees to say the words "sexual harassment." Be an active listener and vigilant in your observations. If they are experiencing a questionable level of discomfort, it is absolutely your business, so don't be afraid to ask questions. Regardless of your personal experience and tolerance and biases, the laws around harassment are very specific, and failure to enforce your company's codes can be costly.

3. EVERYONE IS ENTITLED TO PAID REST AND MEAL BREAKS: FACT OR MYTH?

I was recently reflecting on a speakerphone call I once received from a group of *front-of-house* employees asking, "hypothetically, aren't we entitled to a break and a lunch with pay?" Knowing that such a question is rarely "hypothetical," I provided the standard Department of Labor (DOL) response applicable to that particular state and reiterated the company's break policy but was left with a few of my own questions:

Do I have a manager requiring staff to work through their required breaks? If so, how long has this been going on and how many staff members are affected? Is the manager not familiar with our wage and hour break policies? And if not, what can I do better to make sure that they are?

The call gave me the opportunity to take corrective action, to make sure that our practices aligned with both the law and our company policy. But to my fellow HR leaders, who may be a bit rusty on the labor laws around rest and meal breaks in your state, here is a little oil for that squeak:

To pay or not to pay

Most employers provide paid or unpaid rest and meal breaks. Though this is a common practice, it is not actually required everywhere. While most employers have opted to provide paid or unpaid time for rest and meal breaks, the Fair Labor Standards Act (FLSA) does not require employers to provide rest or meal breaks. Only some states are required to offer rest and meal breaks. Therefore, if your company offers rest or meal breaks, you may not be legally obligated to compensate your employees for that time unless:

the law in your particular state requires paid rest or meal breaks (see "state rest/meal break laws" below)

breaks lasts 20 minutes or less; these shorter breaks are considered part of an employee's workday and must be paid, or your employees have had to work through their break.

Who is entitled to Rest Breaks?

While most employers allow rest breaks in increments of 10 to 15 minutes every 4 hours throughout their shift as a matter of policy, few states actually require employers to offer rest breaks. For laws in your particular state, the Department of Labor provides a list of state rest break laws.

Who is entitled to Meal Breaks?

Again, while a common practice, approximately one-third of states actually require employers to provide a meal break to employees. Where meal breaks are provided, employees who work five to six hours consecutive hours during a shift must be allowed to take at minimum a 30-minute meal break, typically not less than three hours into their shift. For laws in your particular state, the Department of Labor provides a list of state meal break laws.

How to ensure compliance with state labor laws

Laws may change with new political administrations. Stay ahead of the "hypothetical" inquiries by knowing the wage and hour laws for your particular state. Make sure that your employee handbook contains the most up-to-date policy and DOL legislative information on rest and meal breaks in your state.

Require routine wage and hour training of your managers and timekeepers that require them to attest to their participation.

- Conduct periodic internal timekeeping audits for hourly staff to identify compliance gaps.

- Work with managers and staff to ensure that employees who are allowed to take legally required breaks are able to do so, and

- Have documented processes in place for employees who choose to take incremental rest breaks or waive meal breaks in the event of a DOL audit.

- At the end of the day, be mindful when considering your break policies and when in doubt, default to the side of generosity. Your employees will be all the more engaged because of it.

4. CREATING A FAMILY-FRIENDLY CULTURE IS NOT A CHOICE, IT'S THE LAW!

I once boarded a corporate shuttle and happened to sit next to a manager who mentioned he was on his way to terminate an employee's job. When I asked why, he said he needed someone more dependable, someone who didn't "have so many doctor's appointments and family issues."

Something about this offended my Benefit Manager sensibilities. So, I kicked into action. "Tell me more," I asked. As he told the story, I simultaneously texted a member of the HR Benefits team to have them confirm if the ill-fated employee had been, by chance, approved for leave under the Family Medical Leave Act (FMLA) or any other type of leave for that matter. As it happens, she was. Termination averted! Why? Because employees are protected against discrimination for taking unpaid leave under the FMLA. Under FMLA, employers cannot use the taking of a qualified leave as a negative factor in any employment actions, such as promotion, discipline, layoff, or termination unless there is a legitimate non-discriminatory reason for the action.

Family Medical Leave Act… unknown to most, the initial legislation that is now known as the Family Medical Leave Act (FMLA) was drafted by the Women's Legal Defense Fund in 1984. After ten years, it was signed into law in January 1993 under the new Clinton Administration.

Lower your risk by promoting a more family-friendly culture.

This chance encounter on the staff shuttle identified a need for more training and education for managers and timekeepers. Thankfully, I was in the right place at the right time to set right what could have been a significant wrong, a mistake that could have put the company at risk. It was also clear that I needed to work harder to develop a more family-friendly culture as employees struggle to balance the demands of work and caring for themselves and their families.

Ultimately, we all owe gratitude to the tenacious women and men responsible for this law. The first federal law that requires employers with more than 50 employees to guarantee eligible employees a maximum of 12 weeks of unpaid leave each year, without fear of losing their employee benefits or jobs, should they need to take leave for any of the following reasons:

- to care for an immediate family member (spouse, child, or parent) with a serious health condition; to take unpaid medical leave when the employee is unable to work because of a serious health condition, the birth and care of the newborn child of the employee, or placement with the employee of a child for adoption or foster care.

So, how do we build a more family-friendly culture? We should start by training our managers to think more compassionately vs. punitively, how to identify and address a potential leave or accommodation vs. an attendance issue and understand that termination should never be used as a default.

Secondly, direct managers must immediately connect employees with Human Resources (HR) if they have reason to believe that absenteeism or tardiness is linked to a medical issue for the employee or their family. Your HR or Benefits team will collaborate with the employee to determine how to best support them in a way that is both compassionate and compliant during what might be a difficult time. Your HR department has the knowledge and expertise to mitigate risk to the organization by knowing the right legally compliant questions to ask. They can also collaborate with the employee, and internal partners, i.e., payroll and benefits, to determine FMLA eligibility and guide the employee through the confidential certification process.

Educating your managers on the available resources and the compliance rules surrounding them may lower risk and increase employee engagement.

CHAPTER 7

Mental Health

1. MENTAL HEALTH IN THE WORKPLACE IS EVERYONE'S BUSINESS

I was called to a leadership meeting to discuss the next steps following a final warning of a tenured manager for chronic absenteeism, inability to focus and meet deadlines, and unexplained emotional outbursts – all uncustomary behavior for a formerly high-performing manager. Nowhere in previous discussions with the manager was there evidence that anyone had simply asked, "What's happening; how can I support you?" So, I took a shot. I met with the employee and opened the conversation with "What's going on with you? How can we support you?" Through the floodgates came everything from domestic violence to a diagnosed acute mental health condition that had clearly taken its toll on the employee's performance and professional life.

The lesson here was that not all employees experiencing mental health challenges may seek professional help or disclose their condition. It is often left to manifest in the form of poor performance. In this case, the organization offered benefits, along with federally mandated programs, and other resources to support the employee. We simply needed to initiate the discussion.

The exact percentage of employees with mental health issues can vary depending on a number of factors. Based on a study conducted by the National Institute of Mental Health, in 2021, in the United States, there were an estimated 57.8 million people (22.8% of all US adults over the age of 18) suffering from mental ill health. According to the World Health Organization (WHO), it is estimated that one in four people worldwide will experience a mental health condition at some point in their lives. This suggests that a sizable portion of our employees may be affected by mental health issues at any given time.

Because mental health is emerging as a critical concern, organizations are beginning to recognize the impact of a mentally healthy work environment on productivity and engagement; and there is an increasing focus on building awareness and support systems for employees. Mental illness will not only significantly impact your employees but also your organization as a whole. While mental illness may trend higher in specific industries like healthcare, emergency services, and other traditionally high-stress professions, many other factors can lead to elevated levels of mental ill health such as geography, political and economic conditions in the world, and of course the ravages of a pandemic.

Other common factors threatening your employee's mental health in today's workplaces are:

Social isolation in remote workspaces

While remote work offers many advantages to some employees, it can also lead to feelings of social isolation and blurred work-life boundaries, which leads to increased stress, and a lack of social interaction, which can impact the mental health of an employee and their performance.

Work-life imbalance

The expectation of constant availability can stretch the boundaries between work and personal life. Based on statistical data provided by EarthWeb, an online research platform, on average, employees send and receive 126 emails per day. That translates to 126 items of correspondence that require attention at some level which can make balancing work, family, and social commitments challenging. Self-care and mental wellness are rarely considered part of the equation.

Heightened anxiety and depression

Stress in the workplace comes with the territory. However, stress that is overwhelming, prolonged, and impairs daily functioning can lead to anxiety. In addition to heavy workloads and employees adjusting to remote working, there are other factors prevalent in most workplaces such as job insecurity, interpersonal dynamics, and workplace harassment and discrimination, all of which have detrimental effects on your employees' mental health, how they present, and their performance.

The first step in addressing these challenges is recognizing they do exist, and not shying away from the conversation about strategic ways to address them. Start with a comprehensive approach that involves managers and employees. Encourage and train managers to conduct routine one-on-one check-ins with their teams to foster an open dialogue about workload, stress levels, and well-being. This will help reduce the stigma and political incorrectness around mental health. It will also help create a supportive and inclusive environment where employees feel comfortable discussing their concerns without fear of judgment or discrimination.

As tempting as it is to take the 'I don't want to get into anyone's business' approach, mental health, and wellness are at the core of your business and meeting your business objectives. It impacts productivity, job satisfaction, and overall work performance.

Second, train managers to recognize when an employee might be in distress, and how to provide the right resources and support to employees, i.e., Employee Assistance Programs (EAPs), which provide confidential counseling and support services. Know when to engage Human Resources in the use of employee benefits and leave programs to address mental health issues before the damage to the organization and/or an employee's career becomes irreparable.

By building awareness, reducing stigma, and fostering open dialogue about mental health, employers can impact the mental well-being of their workforce and the overall health of their organizations.

2. CONFESSIONS OF A SERIAL WORK SPOUSE

"Work spouse" is a phrase used mostly in American English, referring to a co-worker, usually of the opposite gender, with whom one shares a special relationship, having bonds like those of a marriage. I know this phrase is still considered taboo, but let's be real, we've all used it, and have even had a work spouse. In fact, 23% of workers report that they currently have a work spouse. During my career, I have been graced with some phenomenal work wives. We shared a high level of honesty, mutual respect, loyalty, and trust – and in each case, having that relationship made the workplace safe and palatable under the most toxic of circumstances. The first was Shari, rest her soul; she made standing on my feet for 9 hours a day, selling men's accessories that summer in 1983, seem like summer camp. Then early in my professional career, there was Kevina, an executive assistant who always made sure I received the right intel so that I could be in the right place, at the right time, to be visible for just the right opportunity.

Brenda, Linda, Arlene, Nikki Angela, and Melissa - all created a safe space to vent and made me part of a bigger alliance. I can't forget Theresa, "Tese" who always kept me on my toes with her sharp dry wit, a woman so generous, she would have taken me in if I were homeless.

Ultimately, there was Dawn. It was Dawn who set a standard by which no other work spouse would measure up. Dawn embodied the very definitions of Gallup's "Best Friend" at work. We shared similar values and a keen sense of trust in each other, creating a source of support, safety, and empathic understanding. We could share openly and honestly our likes, dislikes, and observations, strategize about how to get one of us the promotion, cross-check each other, support each other's strengths and weaknesses, help each other cope with stress, and put problems into context. Last but not least, there is Melissa, who is by definition, the consummate 'Ride or Die.'

Work spouse Quiz

- Is there one co-worker above all others that knows your strengths, fears, and weaknesses?

- When something eventful happens at work, is there someone you seek out first and foremost for a de-briefing?

- At meal and coffee breaks, does this co-worker know what to order for you and how you like your coffee (and vice versa)?

- Is there someone in your office who knows almost as much about your personal life as your best friend or real-life spouse does?

If you have answered yes to one or more of these questions – congratulations! May you live happily ever after.

Fun facts about Work Spouses

Employees with work spouses tend to be more engaged in their work and work environments because they tend to feel safer, supported, and therefore more productive compared to employees without the same strong relationships with their colleagues. Work spouses often complement each other in terms of skills, abilities, and approaches to work. Surveys conclude that 70% of employees agree that it is healthy and preferable to have one colleague to confide in and bond with.

In The Five Essential Elements

A New York Times best-seller drawn from Gallup studies – employees who have "a best friend at work" are seven times more likely to be engaged in their jobs, are better at relating to customers, have greater well-being, and are less likely to get injured on the job. Having a great work spouse reduces stress. Who is better to provide reassurance than someone who understands the challenges of one's daily environment? Work spouses also tend to validate each other while providing poignant feedback and coaching based on what they know about each other, both personally and professionally. Work spouses know each other's habits, strengths, and weaknesses; and know where to focus their support. to make a very productive team.

And Now for a Word of Caution

The relationship between work spouses can be misinterpreted. To ensure others are not feeling shut out, remember to promote inclusiveness. Be sure not to isolate others and to solicit feedback and opinions when working on a common initiative. Also, avoid crossing boundaries. It's great to have a support system and a close confidante but be sure to set boundaries for how much to share with your office mate. More importantly, honor those boundaries.

We are with our work families for 8 to 12 hours a day. I've heard the mantra "I don't come to work to make friends," clearly spoken by an individual who has never experienced the benefits of a work spouse. Thank goodness for thought partners to collaborate with in the game of workplace politics.

CHAPTER 8

Leadership

"Sometimes, I feel that we may be a bit
out of touch with our employees."

1. HORRIBLE VS. EXTRAORDINARY BOSSES

I entered my office on Friday to a box on my desk. I assumed it was some equipment from my IT team, but upon further examination I saw it was from a Prime on-line retailer. I opened it to find a personal gift to me from my Chief HR Officer; something not random, but useful; something that aligned with one of my hobbies. It was a great end to an exhausting week. Equally important was the thoughtfulness behind the gift. As I read the gift card, I got all warm and fuzzy, clutched the gift tightly and spun around and around in my chair (figuratively of course) and thought, "what an extraordinary boss"!

This got me thinking about what makes a horrible vs. extraordinary boss. Whenever I tell people I work in Human Resources more often than not they respond, "I don't know how you do it;" As if it's some extraordinary virtue to want to uplift human capital in order to attain the vision of an organization. If I've learned nothing during my HR tours I've learned that employees will only care about your business to the extent that you show that you care about them. Most bosses focus on the general welfare of their organizations but extraordinary bosses care to an exceptional degree about the organization AND the people who work for them.

Since 2000 Gallup reports show that less than one-third of Americans are engaged in their jobs. A more recent Gallup Report State of the American Manager provides a detailed look at the primary characterizations of extraordinary bosses and draws parallels between talent, engagement, job satisfaction and other critical objectives of an organization such as profitability and productivity. Research shows that managers account for as much as 70% of variance in employee engagement scores. Given that consistently for nearly a decade one-third of Americans have been disengaged from their jobs, It's a fair conclusion that most managers are not creating, at a minimum, an environment in which employees feel motivated, much less an environment of comfy coziness. One in two American adults leave their job to get away from their manager thereby improving their quality of life at some point in their career. If you have had the misfortune to be one of those two, you know exactly the situation. A "Horrible Boss" is the kiss of death for productivity, not to mention they make employees feel helpless and undervalued at work which leads to stress and negatively which affects their emotional and often physical wellbeing. So, do you have a horrible boss or two in your midst? Pay attention to what they are doing in the workplace to create but more often, destroy engagement, thereby stagnating the overall level of performance of your business.

In thinking back to past and present bosses, and how effectively they led their organizations to success I have come up the following characterizations and practices of extraordinary bosses:

They encourage autonomy and independence

Engagement and satisfaction are largely based on autonomy, independence and trust.

They strive for a real sense of connection

Admit it, we all work for a paycheck (otherwise we would do volunteer work), but we also want to work for more than a paycheck: we want to work with and for people that we respect and admire–and with and for people who respect and admire us. That's why a kind word, a quick discussion about family, an informal conversation to ask if an employee needs any help–those moments are much more important than meetings or formal evaluations. A true sense of connection is personal, and makes employees feel appreciated and valued.

They set meaningful objectives

Without a meaningful goal to shoot for, work is just work and no one likes work.

They help develop a true sense of purpose – Everyone likes to feel a part of something bigger. Even when it comes to their work lives.

Provide opportunities for significant input – Engaged employees have ideas; disregard their ideas without consideration, they immediately disengage. It's just that simple.

They help develop a meaningful future

To expect someone to work without the possibility of personal betterment is the very definition of slavery, and where did that get us? Every job should have the potential to lead to greater things. Extraordinary bosses take time to develop employees for the jobs they someday hope to have, even if the job is with another organization.

They set clear goals and expectations

While every job should include some degree of independence, everyone needs a little guidance.

They give private criticism

Extraordinary bosses always do it in private. Rule #1. Never yell at or talk down to a subordinate, publicly or privately.

They give public praise

Public praise does not a weak boss make. You might have to work hard to find reasons to recognize an employee who simply meets standards, but that's OK: A few words of recognition—especially public recognition—may be the nudge an average performer needs to start becoming a great performer.

They Care

It doesn't mean you are not about business. It means you recognize that people are the business. Extraordinary bosses have the talent to motivate employees and build genuine relationships. Those who are not well-suited for the job will likely be uncomfortable with this "soft" aspect of leadership. Extraordinary bosses take time to know and understand their employees as people so that they can motivate them to become high performers.

Employees are prepared to give their ALL to your organization which is what you need to reach your goals. But none of this can happen if employees do not feel valued or cared about. If bosses in your organization struggle with what is considered the soft aspects of leadership, checking your engagement scores, you may find that they are not suited for the role.

2. HOLISTIC LEADERSHIP DURING COVID, POLITICS, AND QUITE FRANKLY EVERYTHING ELSE

Lately we've been stressed with a mixture of first world problems, Black people problems, COVID concerns – you name it. There still seems to be the open-ended question if or not Black Lives Matter. I'm fearful for my Gen-Z and Millennial nephews out in the world, trying to survive something akin to hunting season. I'm worried about the future or our democracy, my own personal freedom, and now with the passing of the Honorable Ruth Bader Ginsberg, I'm concern about the liberties and freedoms of the women that I know and love, as well as myself. All of which could impact how I show up to work, my staff, and the community that we serve. All that aside, I got up, this morning, got ready for work, and logged onto the all-staff meeting with my best Zoom smile.

But this was not your typical all-staff meeting where the leader without so much as a "good morning" immediately launches into the "what have you done for me lately" portion of the meeting. No: the Executive Director opened first and foremost with a smile, followed by a wellness check of her staff. Why? Because clearly this was a leader that knows that simply *recognizing* stress in the workplace can go a long way in making your employees feel seen and heard. She didn't ignore it, but she acknowledged what was happening in world of pandemics and politics, right during one of the most impactful periods of social unrest since the civil right movement.

The leader made what was most certainly the source of anxiety and concern for most of her staff a part of the business initiative to be discussed, rather than isolated as something personal to be dealt with in your own time. With empathy and compassion, she provided some coping resources and a safe space to feel and be supported by a largely remote staff, some of which are working in isolation. In a world where caring for the people responsible for the success of your organization is considered *Muda* (Lean speak for waste), it was refreshing to see it as a core part of the agenda.

With the reality of living in the midst of a pandemic and chaos of national proportions, without the ability to take proper respite from it due to unprecedented travel and health risk, and being essentially geographically sequestered, it's safe to say life is complicated. Add to the mix 13,000,000 neighbors, family members, colleagues, and friends unemployed and the uncertain future for many other jobs and businesses as we approach election and holiday season, and it gets even more complex.

Your employees may not have asked for it, and likely don't expect it, but they are equally likely in need of extra support. When times are tough and your employees are on edge, managers need to understand that stress can manifest itself in performance and how employee *"shows up."* Dedicating time to connect more informally with your employees either individually or as a group to find out what each needs stay engaged, focused and motivated can be a good investment of your time both in establishing trust as a leader, and maintaining productivity for your organization. For leaders that struggle with the concept of people first, I recommend you explore the possibilities with the following 3 tips supporting your organizing through stressful periods:

1. **Recognize your employees for their hard work**
   It's time to get proactive. Every single person is juggling as much as - if not more than - they can bear. The complexity of 2020 continues to impact all of us. Your employees may not feel okay expressing the strain they are under. The best thing to do first is to acknowledge the stress factors as

well as workloads, without having it specifically laid out for you to react to. Hard work that continues to go unnoticed will only compound the stress. In addition to calling out the stress and making it making resources available to mitigate it, be sure to show gratitude and appreciation for the contributions of your employees in more formal programs. Make sure they know you get it.

2. **Make sure you know what's going on with your team. Surprises are usually best left to board games. Don't just check-in, check-up. Transform 1:1's. with questions like:**
   - What have you done that you're proud of since we last spoke?
   - What's been your biggest source of frustration here or otherwise?
   - Is there anything that I can do more or less of to make your work life a little less stressful?

Their answers will give you an accurate read on what's going well, what they enjoy, and what might be adding to their stress at work. These are the types of things you need to have on your radar. They matter.

3. **Leverage your internal partnerships**
   Stonehenge, despite rumors of giants in the Earth, is simply an example of what humans can

do when they team together, when they organize well.

In times of stress and uncertainty, many leaders attempt take on the task of managing everything themselves - attempting to lift massive obelisks with their bare hands. In reality, it's key to understand the strengths of your internal partners, and know when to leverage them. As one example, devising and implementing solutions to support the organization and its employees is critical right now. You may lack the skills to build those. Partner with your Human Resources and Organizational Development teams here. They'll help you establish a relationship of trust and partnership that ensure that your human capital is always engaged and emotionally fit for duty.

"Always be known for helping someone"

-Jennifer McClure